AEROSMITH

A Band Like No Other

James Court

NEW HAVEN PUBLISHING LTD

First Edition
Published 2019
NEW HAVEN PUBLISHING LTD
www.newhavenpublishingltd.com
newhavenpublishing@gmail.com

Cover design ©Pete Cunliffe
pcunliffe@blueyonder.co.uk

newhaven
publishing

ISBN: 978-1-912587-27-8

Content

A Band Like No Other

Aerosmith are without doubt the ultimate in everything that a rock band should be. They represent the pinnacle in hell-raising glory and bona fide rock exuberance. They are the blueprint for the signature rock band - how it should sound, how it should look, and how it should behave; an absolute raw force with pure organic foundations in blues and rock psychedelia. There is simply no rock band around that qualifies more ultimately than Aerosmith to stand alone at the pinnacle of all things that are defined as rock and roll.

The band's early influences of The Beatles, The Rolling Stones, The Yardbirds, The New York Dolls and Led Zeppelin gave them an incredible foundation to develop their own individual standing in this competitive arena of performance and rock notoriety. In fact, they would go on to be just as influential themselves as the bands that initially influenced them in these early days. The band was fused together on these great imprints and they effortlessly and skilfully entwined these sounds, those of the standard high-profile rock bands of the time, creating a unique and captivating rawness.

Future bands such as Nirvana, Guns N' Roses, Motley Crew, Metallica, Skid Row, Extreme and many more were highly influenced by the singular and incomparable nature of the early songs and performances they would sustain. Aerosmith had great strength within the band, and not just in the brilliant captivating live performances, but in the fact that the band members equally shared the songwriting credits as a collective, giving a new element to each and every album. In addition - and this is key - they were visually an incredible unit. They lived to excess, pushing the boundaries of sex, drugs and rock and roll to the edge and beyond. It's a legacy that all great rock bands have in some form but at no

5

point did the music ostensibly suffer; in fact it could be argued that it was indeed enhanced. There was incredible musicianship within the core of the band with particular attention given to the chemistry and musical synergy between Joe Perry and Brad Whitford, and of course to the captivating front man and incredible vocals of Steven Tyler. They were, in short, an absolute force to be reckoned with.

These core members of Steven Tyler (1970-present), Tom Hamilton (1970-present), Joey Kramer (1970-present), Joe Perry (1970-1979, 1984-present) and Brad Whitford (1971-1981, 1984-present) have maintained the Aerosmith legacy. Early members also included Ray Tabana who from 1970-1971 played rhythm and lead guitar, Jimmy Crespo who played guitar from 1979-1984 and Rick Dufay who was with the band as a guitarist for three years from 1981 through to 1984. Aerosmith are a band that fully encompass all that everyone loves in a rock and roll band. They are flamboyant, they have swagger, they are excessive, they write great rock music, put on electrifying live performances and have an incredible enigmatic lead singer.

They of course were not alone in the extravagance of the early days; many bands around in the 1970s were excessive in the lifestyles they led, but none were more so than Aerosmith. It was here that they stood alone. Drugs and its consumption were an ongoing issue, or not an issue, as some would point out. They pushed the limits here more than most; they had incredible wealth, private planes, cars, women and any indulgence they desired. Noted amongst this period were the 1976 *Rocks* and the 1977 *Draw the Line* recordings which were particularly highlighted for substance extravagance and exuberance. The resources that that the band had were literally limitless and, while other bands like Zeppelin and The Stones had an element of control, Aerosmith famously didn't. They were without doubt the most potent and excessive rock band of the era.

But even behind all the past excess they returned each time stronger than ever, moving forward and remaining at the forefront of cross overs in to other areas of music and society, notably hip hop and rock balladry, and it's this that makes them more than standard rock stars; this makes them culturally significant as well, defining them into a legendary status. Today they have a back

6

catalogue of truly remarkable songs that will forever make them current and on trend; they have worked through the years tirelessly and emerged with a legacy that will be of inspiration for decades into the future.

They have for over 40 years remained a symbolic and significant rock band, changing and adapting as the years progressed but equally staying true to what they ultimately are. Remaining fundamentally undiluted and musically cutting edge, they are organic and unprocessed, primitive and raw. The ultimate Rock Gods. This is their remarkable story.

Formation

Steven Victor Tallarico, later Steven Tyler, was born on March 26th 1948, at the Polyclinic Hospital Manhattan in New York. He was a second child, having an older sister, Lynda Tallarico. Steven's father, Victor A. Tallarico, was of German and Italian descent, and he was a classical musician and pianist who taught music at the Cardinal Spellman High School, which was within the Bronx district of the city. Steven's mother was born Susan Ray Blancha and she mostly lived in Nashua Hunt Community. In 1945 Susan and Victor met and they eventually married. They had just the two children, firstly Lynda and then Steven. Steven's mother had many talented friends, like musicians and painters, and she even made oil paintings herself. The family later moved to the Bronx area when Steven was around three years old. Steven, his older sister and his parents stayed in the Bronx district for around five years until they again moved home, this time to Yonkers when Steven was around nine. Later Steven's mother and father ran a summer resort which they named 'Trow-Rico', situated in New Hampshire. The name derived from Trow Hill, which was a local landmark, and the family name Tallerico. The resort was situated within woods and fields and consisted of cottages in acres of peaceful surroundings; this would be where the family would spend their summers. Steven had the touring and performing DNA firmly set: his grandfather had arrived in the USA from Italy in the 1920s alongside four brothers, and the youngest of the four, Pasquale, was reportedly a child prodigy on the piano while Fransesco and Giovanni played the mandolin, and the fourth brother, Michael, played guitar. They named themselves The

Tallerico Brothers and toured and performed in areas such as Detroit and Connecticut.

In Yonkers Steven attended Roosevelt High School. His bad boy future self however was starting to develop, and he was expelled for allegedly taking drugs. With music very much the driving factor in Steven's young life he nevertheless graduated from his next school, the Quintano's school for Young Professionals. The school today is no longer in existence but the original building was located on 45th Street between 8th and 9th Avenues. The name Quintano's is still on the outside of the building. It closed when Dr. Quintano himself died.

Now determined to pursue a career in music, the 16-year-old Steven Tallerico formed his first band in 1964, The Strangers. At this point however he was not the full front man that would dominate the stage in the years ahead; here he opted instead to be the band's drummer, sharing the vocals. Also, on discovering that there was another band with the same name on the circuit they quickly opted for a change of name, and The Strangers became The Strangeurs. The Strangeurs consisted of Steven Tallarico on drums and vocals, Peter Stahl on guitar, Alan Strohmayer on bass, Don Solomon on keyboards and vocals and Barry Shapiro, who also played drums. During initial performances the band decided to have a rethink of the line-up, which resulted in Steven Tallarico now taking the central role of lead vocals while also playing harmonica and percussion, with Peter Stahl on guitar, Alan Strohmayer on bass, Don Sloan, formerly Don Solomon, on keyboards and Barry Shore, formerly Barry Shapiro, on drums. The reshuffle also prompted another name change now that Steven was the full front man, and The Strangeurs now became Chain Reaction. Chain Reaction toured the circuit and released two singles of their own: 'The Sun' / 'When I Needed You' in 1966 and 'You Should Have Been Here Yesterday' / 'Ever Lovin' Man' later in 1968. They supported many large bands including The Beach Boys, The Byrds and The Yardbirds and followed a more pop psychedelia sound than that of pure rock. The band was now starting to gain attention while on the circuit, which would lead to a significant meeting when Chain Reaction was billed on the same night as another band called The Jam Band, commonly known as

9

Joe Perry's Jam Band; within this band was of course the young Joe Perry himself.

Anthony Joseph Perry was born in Lawrence, Massachusetts and grew up in the town of Hopedale, Massachusetts. At a young age Joe struggled in school academically. He had dreams of becoming a marine biologist and was fascinated by Jacques Cousteau, the French naval officer, explorer, conservationist, filmmaker, scientist, photographer and researcher, who studied the sea and all forms of life in water. His grades however were not good enough and his career aspirations were looking doubtful. Eventually his parents removed him from the school and he joined an all-boys preparatory school, Vermont Academy, which was a boarding school located in a small town in Vermont called Saxton's River. The school boarded up to 200 boys. Joe actually suffered from ADHD, but at this time, when he was a teenager, it was not heard of and undiagnosed, and as a result he was seen more as a slow learner with a discipline problem. The condition however drew his focus to the guitar, and Joe started to realise that it actually helped him play, and also helped his retention in remembering things on the instrument; here he had a natural ability that he could develop. In short, the guitar was one place where he had no issue at all. The school itself was also an eyeopener for Joe. His parents' views on the school and the way they perceived it to help his learning were vastly different to what Joe actually experienced. Until this point Joe had led a relatively sheltered life in a small town. The school was a mix of kids from all over the US, many from huge cities, and after holiday breaks they would return with new and exciting stories that gave Joe a new perspective on the world and a new exposure. This was in the middle of the 1960s era of sex, drugs and rock and roll, and it would set Joe on a completely different path to what was initially planned; in fact the career Joe would end up in couldn't have been further from the initial direction the school was intended to give him. Joe discovered *The Village Voice*, which was first real newspaper that went under the radar to cover culture in the US, and it was here that Joe discovered the music scene sweeping through. It started for him with The Beatles, when, like millions of Americans, he witnessed the band on *The Ed Sullivan Show*. This was something that nobody had really seen before and for the young Joe it was captivating: the way they looked, the way the sounded - he was mesmerised by it; it changed him completely and changed the direction he was heading into. He now became obsessed with playing, constantly copying music on records and returning the needle to certain points so he could play along, perfecting the riffs. Here he discovered other major influences in music at the time, notably Jimi Hendrix, The Who, The Kinks, and The Yardbirds, who would be responsible for one of Aerosmith's most famous covers, 'Train Kept a Rollin'.

After school Joe Perry set himself up with a band after he had met bass player Tom Hamilton. They named the band simply the Jam Band, playing mainly free form blues and blues itself. In September 1969 Joe and Tom moved to Boston, Massachusetts and it was here that they met a drummer who was from the Yonkers area called Joey Kramer. At this time Joey Kramer was actually attending Berklee College of Music as a student but decided to drop out to join the Jam Band. It was Joey Kramer who knew about Steven Tyler and always had aspirations of joining him in some form.

At this time, while playing the circuit, it was at a gig in 1970 that the future 'Bad Boys from Boston' played at the same gig. Chain Reaction and Jam Band watched each other with interest. Steven Tyler immediately loved the sound of Jam Band and made a proposal to combine the two bands together.

A month later the two bands met up again, in October 1970, and talked through the proposition of bringing the two bands together. Steven Tyler at this point was still a backup singer rather than complete frontman in Chain Reaction, but he now refused to be put behind the drums and insisted on being the lead singer and frontman. The other members of the band all agreed and the new band was instantly formed. They set up home together in Boston, at 1325 Commonwealth Avenue, and here they rehearsed and wrote music together and took time out between performing at various early shows. They also allegedly started dabbling in drugs and would reportedly watch shows such as *The Three Stooges* while getting stoned. The band at this point still didn't have an agreed name but Joey Kramer had a school notebook, and all over it he would write the word 'Aerosmith', the name having reportedly come to him while he was listening to Harry Nilsson's album *Aerial Ballet*. The album was the third studio album by Harry Nilsson and was released in 1968. The album cover had an art drawing of a circus performer jumping out of a biplane; this was also the inspiration for the wing's motif. It was initially rejected but the band thought it was 'Arrowsmith'; when Joey Kramer explained the correct spelling it was shortlisted with some other names (one was 'The Hookers'), and later it was agreed.

The band still needed an additional guitarist, more of a rhythm guitarist, and Steven recommended a childhood friend of his named Ray Tabano. The band was now complete: Steven Tyler, Ray Tabano, Joey Kramer and Joe Perry. After many more rehearsals Aerosmith played their first gig in Mendon, Massachusetts at Nipmuc Regional High School, on November 6, 1970. The school is now Miscoe Hill Middle School. In 1971, Tabano was replaced by Brad Whitford, who also attended the Berklee School of Music. Brad Whitford was experienced even at this point in time, as he was formerly a member of the band Earth Inc. It was on August 24th 1971 at The Savage Beast in Vermont that the band had its first show with Brad Whitford, and from there on the band played a series of gigs at colleges, high schools, junior high schools, clubs, ballrooms, and other small venues throughout New England and New York. Other than for a period from July 1979 to April 1984, this line-up of Tyler, Perry, Hamilton, Kramer, and Whitford stayed the same. The bad boys from Boston had finally arrived and now started their rise to becoming one of rock's most influential and cutting-edge bands. It was time to get a record deal.

Early Years 1971-1975

Aerosmith's first live shows consisted mainly of covers, which was not uncommon around this time, particularly for a new band working the circuit. The shows followed roughly the following set list: 'Route 66', 'Rattlesnake Shake', 'Happenings Ten Years' Time Ago', 'Movin' Out', 'Somebody', 'Think About It', 'Walkin' the Dog', 'Live with Me', 'Great Balls of Fire', 'Good Times Bad Times'. Although the band were playing small venues made up of various town halls, YMCAs and high schools, they were not the average standard rock outfit and anyone watching knew they were something different, something special. Through November and December 1970, and into the start of 1971, they quickly became noticed and were getting attention as a formidable live unit. The band worked through an agency at the time, the Ed Malhoit Agency, which handled all their bookings. Looking to progress further they signed a promotion deal with Frank Connelly, and eventually secured a management deal with David Krebs and Steve Leber in 1972. Frank Connelly had previously heard a demo tape of the band and Steve Leber at this time was the head of the music division of the William Morris Agency, and he agreed to bring Aerosmith to Max's Kansas City and showcase them. Invited to the gig were Ahmet Ertegun, chairman of Atlantic Records, and Clive Davis, who at the time was president of Columbia Records. Steve Leber himself would go on to run his own management company, Contemporary Communications Corp, and managed artists like The Rolling Stones, Simon & Garfunkel, and Def Leppard.

Aerosmith to this point had played dozens of shows all through 1971 and into 1972. The gig at Max's Kansas City however was different: two future heavyweights in the record industry were there, and both Clive Davis and Ahmet Ertegun watched with interest. Ahmet Ertegun would be best known as the co-founder and president of Atlantic Records; throughout his career he discovered and developed many leading rhythm and blues and rock musicians. He also wrote classic blues and pop songs. In addition, he served as the chairman of the Rock and Roll Hall of Fame and museum which is located in Cleveland, Ohio. He would often be described as one of the most significant figures in the modern recording industry and later, in 2017, he was inducted into Rhythm & Blues Hall of Fame in recognition of his work in the music business. Equally Clive Davis was just as influential: he had been the president of Columbia Records since 1967 and would remain so until 1973. Later he founded and became president of Arista Records from 1975 through to 2000 until founding J Records. Clive Davis was always credited with hiring young up and coming recording artists. He nurtured many that would go on to be superstars in their own right, these including Janis Joplin, Santana, Bruce Springsteen, Chicago, Billy Joel, Pink Floyd, and of course the now soon to be signed Aerosmith. The venue, Max's Kansas City, where Aerosmith performed that evening was a nightclub and restaurant which became a renowned gathering spot for musicians, poets, artists and politicians throughout the 1960s and 1970s. It was opened by Mickey Ruskin in December 1965, and closed in 1981. On the evening in question Aerosmith were not scheduled to actually play, and they paid out of their own pockets to be allowed to perform. They would later write the song 'No Surprize' which was in connection to this moment, and the track appeared on the album *Night in the Ruts* released later in 1979. Naturally, the gig was a success. Aerosmith signed to Columbia in 1972 and immediately began working on their debut album.

The group recorded their debut album at Intermedia Studios at 331 Newbury Street, Boston, Massachusetts with record producer Adrian Barber. The album and its creation would stand as a huge learning curve for the new band who were complete novices in the studio at this time. Adrian Barber had moved into production in the late 1960s, becoming a recording engineer and producer for Atlantic Records. He had worked throughout 1969

14

with Cream on *Goodbye*, The Allman Brothers Band, Velvet Underground's *Loaded* while also drumming on two tracks, The Rascals' *Freedom Suite*, Bee Gees' *Odessa* and many more before agreeing to work with the new band recently signed, Aerosmith. The band on reflection were not complimentary to the producer and were unhappy with the sound; they were however not in a position to dictate and didn't have enough experience, or knowledge, to argue the case. Steven Tyler, through his own nervousness and insecurity, changed his voice on the record when the red light finally came on; he wasn't comfortable with the way he sounded when recording started and he wanted to sound more like a blues singer. He does sound completely different on the record compared to the famous vocal style he would later be renowned for. Joe Perry was also unhappy with how things went; he thought the band were better than they were portrayed on the record and thought the producer made a poor job in the overall sound that was coming through. His guitar was not cutting through the music as he had wanted: even though he felt that he was playing well, it wasn't represented through the production. But again, the band kept quiet even though they were troubled by the sound. Tom Hamilton also had similar feelings and felt that the album was recorded so fast it left little time for anything else; he admits he can hardly recall anything apart from some overdubbing. In short, they didn't, yet, have the full identity they would soon uncover, and were inexperienced in every conceivable way in the studio; that said, the basis for what was to come was there and the rise to become one the biggest American rock bands of the 1970s was well and truly under way.

The self-titled debut album was released on January 5th 1973 with the final track listing as: 'Make It', 'Somebody', 'Dream On', 'One Way Street', 'Mama Kin', 'Write Me a Letter', 'Movin' Out' and 'Walkin' the Dog'. Steven Tyler performed the lead vocals, and played harmonica and wood flute, Joe Perry played lead guitar and sang backup vocals while Brad Whitford played rhythm guitar. On bass was Tom Hamilton and Joey Kramer played drums. An additional musician was David Woodford, who played saxophone on 'Mama Kin' and 'Write Me'. The tracks all have a mixture of influences attributed to them, and came through

15

different experiences, dreams, aspirations and in some cases simply playing until a riff or 'lick' was found. The band at this point had already played hundreds of gigs and sometimes even two or three per evening. 'Make It' was a song Steven Tyler wrote when he was thinking about what would be the perfect song to open for The Rolling Stones, and the track 'Somebody' was based around a section that one of the roadies of the band used to play; Steven took it and added lyrics. The song 'Dream On' had been around for quite a while, at least four years before the band actually formed, Steven wrote it when he was around 17 years old on a Steinway upright piano while he was at Trow-Rico Lodge. The following track, 'One Way Street', was again written on the piano but had the rhythm and the harp coming from 'Midnight Rambler'. Again Steven Tyler's love of music provided inspiration and a basis for riffs; the track 'Mama Kin' was written on an old guitar that was found in the garbage on the street, and the opening of the track was borrowed from an old song by Blodwyn Pig, the British blues rock band, founded in 1968 by guitarist–vocalist–songwriter Mick Abrahams. 'Write Me a Letter' was originally called 'Bite Me' and had been in development for many months, but wasn't feeling quite right at the time; something was missing, and then one day it all seemed to come together when Joey Kramer gave it a different rhythm and it quickly fell into place. 'Movin' Out' was the first song that Steven Tyler wrote with Joe Perry, whereas the final track on the album, 'Walkin' the Dog', is a cover of the Rufus Thomas song. It was first released on his 1963 album of the same name and became his signature hit. It was also his biggest, reaching number ten on the Billboard Hot 100 in December 1963 and remaining on the Hot 100 for 14 weeks. Many bands had up to this point covered the track including The Rolling Stones in 1964; it was the final track on their debut album released on 16 April 1964. The self-titled album was released by Decca Records in the UK but for America had a different track list; this was released on London Records on 30th May 1964, subtitled *England's Newest Hit Makers*, which later became its official title.

A week after the release of the album the first ever single from Aerosmith was released. 'Mama Kin' was released on January 13th 1973. It failed to make any real chart success but

16

would go on to be a staple amongst the Aerosmith live offering and a significant track on future live and compilation albums. It appeared on the live albums *Live! Bootleg*, *Classics Live* and *A Little South of Sanity*. In addition, the song also appeared on several future Aerosmith compilations including *Gems* (1988), *Pandora's Box* (1991), *Pandora's Toys* (1995), *'O, Yeah!' Ultimate Aerosmith Hits* (2002), *Greatest Hits 1973–1988* (2004), and *Devil's Got a New Disguise* from 2006.

The album itself wasn't the classic album the band had hoped it would be, and the sales reflected this. It did however have plenty of highlights scattered all the way through it and, as an album to revisit, the foundations of the future are well and truly laid down. The music is pure and driven and encompasses all that was great in the early sound of a 1970s rock and roll record. The band also had competition on the live circuit, and they were heavily compared to the New York Dolls at this time, and of course the Stones. Critics often wrote that they could not really tell them apart, with the three front men all having similar visual attributes. Unlike the New York Dolls however, Aerosmith would have longevity; the New York Dolls would fall away very quickly in the years ahead, imploding on their own early success, but at this time they were very much on the rise; and of course The Rolling Stones were well and truly stamping their authority. Aerosmith on this first album release and in the shows they gave were nearly always compared to the other rock bands they were sounding similar to: their unique signature sound was not yet developed, on record anyway, but it was coming. They would go on to be one of most successful bands of the next two decades. Steven Tyler, Joe Perry, Brad Whitford, Tom Hamilton and Joey Kramer had hammered their sound into shape over many months of performing and rehearsing, and even though their debut album had not fully represented them as they would have wanted, they were well and truly on their way.

Aerosmith eventually peaked at number 166 with the highest-charting single from the album, 'Dream On', peaking at number 59. Again, the album gave way to several staples for the band's live shows, notably 'Mama Kin' and 'Walkin' the Dog'. They also received plenty of airplay on rock radio stations, given them more exposure. As with all bands with longevity, the album was returned to after the later success of future albums, resulting in it eventually reaching gold status: it rose to sell two million copies and went even further by being certified double platinum after the band reached mainstream success over a decade later.

Throughout the rest of 1973 Aerosmith toured and performed constantly, mostly in New England. In October of this year they had a small breakthrough when they landed some nationwide exposure. They opened for Mott the Hoople, who had had recent success with the Bowie penned 'All The Young Dudes' taken from their 1972 album of the same name; it was a good boost, and they next headed into the studio to work on their second album.

In December of this year they booked themselves into the Record Plant in New York City to record their second album *Get Your Wings*. The record was recorded from December 1973 through to March 1974. The band were unhappy with the production on their first record so a new producer was very much on the agenda. *Get Your Wings* was the first record that would be produced by Jack Douglas, who would continue to work with the band over the coming years. Jack Douglas started at the Record Plant as a janitor, but soon worked his way up to the recording desk as a recording engineer. Here he worked with Miles Davis and many others before he was given the opportunity to assist in engineering The Who's 1971 Record Plant sessions for the *Lifehouse* project. Although the project was later cancelled the initial conception was a science fiction rock opera which was intended as a follow-up to *Tommy*. It was abandoned as a rock opera in favour of creating the traditional rock album *Who's Next*, also in 1971. The songs that were recorded however went on to appear on various albums and singles by The Who, as well as some of Pete Townshend's solo albums. Jack Douglas also went on to work with John Lennon around this time on the classic *Imagine* album and he formed a close bond with Lennon, working with him over the years ahead. Moving into producing he had recently worked on The New York Dolls' self-titled debut album *The New York Dolls* recorded in April 1973 and released in July. It was here he made the move more permanently from an engineer to a producer. With a background as an engineer and now having produced a rock album he was the right choice for Aerosmith at exactly the right time.

The album had Joey Kramer on drums and percussion, Tom Hamilton on bass and Brad Whitford on electric guitar. Joe Perry played electric guitar, twelve-string guitar, slide guitar and acoustic guitar and Steven Tyler performed the lead vocals and harmonica. The record was engineered by Jack Douglas, Jay Messina and Rod O'Brien, and it was produced by Jack Douglas with Ray Colcord. The tracks themselves also had additional personnel on some of the songs: 'Same Old Song And Dance' had baritone saxophone played by Stan Bronstein, tenor saxophone by Michael Brecker, trombone by Jon Pearson and trumpet by Randy Brecker. 'Lord Of The Thighs' had additional piano by Steven Tyler while 'Spaced' had keyboards played by Ray Colcord. 'Woman Of The World', 'S.O.S. (Too Bad)' and 'Train Kept A Rollin' had the main band only while 'Seasons Of Wither' had Steven Tyler adding acoustic guitar. On 'Pandora's Box' he also played piano with Stan Bronstein playing baritone saxophone, and there was also tenor saxophone on the track which was performed by Michael Brecker.

Get Your Wings was released on March 1st 1974 on Columbia and it's here that we see the band really starting to own their classic 1970s rock sound. This was evident in the new production on the record provided by Jack Douglas, and he would go on in the years ahead to produce a total of seven albums with the group. The sound is what the band wanted and the production captures the foundations of the band more accurately; the balance is found in the studio to develop the bridge between blues and rock 'n' roll, and this would be the platform to help launch the group into the mainstream for the first time. Here the band are at a turning point, hinting at what they would be later in the 1980s but still keeping the raw rock sound of their early days. Steven Tyler wrote three songs solo and co-wrote every other song with the exception of the album's single cover song. This was an album that also showcased the skills and union between guitarists Joe Perry and Brad Whitford, happily trading lead and rhythm elements throughout the album and seamlessly switching between blues-rock and the more standard hard rock that was around at the time.

Again, comparisons were made to similar bands on the circuit; in this case reviews often cited them as clones of the Rolling Stones but this was easily written and not accurate. Aerosmith were on their own track and were looking like they were moving in their own inevitable direction towards rock dominance.

Again, following the album future concert staples were born, adding to the touring canon of the band. On side one 'Same Old Song and Dance', built around a Joe Perry guitar riff, gave them only a minor hit in the short term but translated perfectly to the live listing of the band with its interspersed horns and tenor saxophone. 'Lord of the Thighs' showcases a solid drum beat by Joey Kramer pushing the intro forward and the track builds well with each instrument coming in turn. Steven Tyler's vocals are bluesy and deep, taking the song through three phases ending with Joe Perry's riff-infused outro with several effect-rich overdubs. The song was the last recorded for the album; the band needed just one more and they bedded down in the studio working through the track. 'Women of the World' was a song that Steven Tyler had around for a while; in fact it dates back to the mid-sixties when he was with his former band The Strangeurs. It was co-written by then-band-mate Don Solomon and it follows a similar pattern to 'Lord of the Thighs' before branching away into effective melodies and potent riffing. It has an almost jam session feeling to the ending of the song, with a harmonica solo by Steven Tyler sandwiched between guitar leads by Perry and Whitford.

The second side of *Get Your Wings* showcases a more raw edge and kicks off with 'S.O.S. (Too Bad)' which brings some loose sleaze that would also appear later on albums such as *Draw the Line*. It's basically a hard rock song, short and full of energy - an area that punk would later move into. The album's only cover, 'Train Kept A-Rollin', allegedly caused issues between the new producer and the band; it blended two different versions together at different tempos, putting them together back to back and also adding in some live elements, and the band were reportedly unhappy with the method; in addition the producer had two session guitarists playing respective halves of the song. The added crowd noise at the end of the track was treated and synthesised to create a wind type effect, and this then blended into a segue for the next song. Many believe that the next track, 'Seasons of Wither', is one of the finest of all Aerosmith songs and it's a great early showcase of Steven Tyler's eerie vocal melodies that fit perfectly with the feel and presentation of the song. The track speaks of scenery and is deeply descriptive, making it both compelling and romantic in delivery, and it finishes very strongly. It is a definitive highlight on the album. Drummer Joey Kramer has a credit for the final track on the album, 'Pandora's Box'; it's a classic rock and soul track, providing a brass section similar to the album's opener 'Same Old Song and Dance'. The song was reportedly inspired by 1960s Motown and blue-eyed soul.

Get Your Wings was a big disappointment at the time for the band. They felt they were on to something special, and they were right to feel that way: the album was full of quality and should have performed better than it did. The facts were though that it only reached number 74 on the album charts. It was only a matter of time however, because going forward, as with the debut album, it would become extremely popular and eventually would sell over three million. The album well and truly proved to be the starting point for their greatest run of quality albums.

From here Aerosmith would hit the road again and continue to establish themselves as a truly incredible live band. Throughout all of 1974 they toured, and toured constantly. They performed shows night after night, perfecting their live offering and gaining a formidable reputation, on and off the stage in every rock and roll way possible. Their fanbase was growing, and growing rapidly, which would give them the perfect storm; and the next album release would transform them into full on international rock stars. The band had essentially now turned a corner and the breakthrough they had been working so hard to accomplish had now arrived. The bad boys from Boston were about to go from boys to toys.

Sweet Breakthrough

Looking back at the evolution of Aerosmith from their early foundations on to the first couple of albums, it was inevitable that the breakthrough was coming. The *Get Your Wings* tour in support of the album was already establishing them as a force to reckoned with when performing live, and the indulgences and excess they were now taking as part of this experience was already getting them a formidable reputation. The tour of the USA took in over 90 dates from January 1974 through to December 1974 before they returned to the studio in January 1975 to record *Toys in the Attic* through to March.

The album well and truly set the style and the sound of hard rock and heavy metal for the next two decades for the band. Here they were unashamedly raunchy and had that bluesy swagger. The past comparisons to the Rolling Stones and the New York Dolls would now fade away as Aerosmith found their own sound and identity. They found the line between what was the attitude of the Rolling Stones and the over-camped flamboyance of the New York Dolls. They had developed through their own shows and song writing a very lean, raw and dirty riff-oriented rock band that was loose and engaging. *Toys in the Attic* gave them a cutting edge.

At the time they started to record *Toys in the Attic* they had honed all their skills as a live band, and they had developed into a sleek, hard-driving hard rock outfit powered by simple, almost brutal, blues-based riffs. It's this that made the album such a breakthrough success both commercially and artistically. They were now suddenly seen as an individual band, almost punk in presentation. They didn't conform to Led Zeppelin's arty exaggerations and avoided the rock gloom of Black Sabbath;

instead they developed their own place between them all, and essentially owned it. It was all stripped back, raw and to the core, a riff based sound that pulled rock and roll to the extreme. Steven Tyler's lyrics were full of jokes and double entendres and visually the whole band as a collective had a streetwise charm. They basically separated themselves completely from the heavy, lumbering arena rockers of the era. *Toys in the Attic* showed that Aerosmith were a unique and talented band in their own right.

The album was released on April 8th 1975 with a track listing as follows: side one: 'Toys in the Attic' written by Steven Tyler and Joe Perry, 'Uncle Salty' written by Steven Tyler and Tom Hamilton, 'Adam's Apple' written by Steven Tyler, 'Walk This Way' written by Steven Tyler and Joe Perry and 'Big Ten Inch Record' written by Fred Weismantel. Side two started with 'Sweet Emotion' written by Steven Tyler and Tom Hamilton, then 'No More No More' written by Steven Tyler and Joe Perry, 'Round and Round' written by Steven Tyler and Brad Whitford and finally 'You See Me Crying' written by Steven Tyler and Don Solomon. There were a couple of additional musicians on the record: Scott Cushnie played piano on 'Big Ten Inch Record' and 'No More No More' with Jay Messina adding some bass marimba on 'Sweet Emotion'. The record was again produced by Jack Douglas. 'Sweet Emotion' was released in May 1975 and became the band's first real hit single, breaking into the Top 40 in the summer of 1975. The album took a steady climb and peaked at number 11 shortly afterward. With this success in mind it was time to capitalise and show that Aerosmith had two other albums on the market; this prompted the re-release of the power ballad 'Dream On' which now rose fast and reached the Top 10 in early 1976. Both *Aerosmith* (the debut album) and *Get Your Wings* climbed back up the charts strongly in the wake of *Toys in the Attic*.

The second single released from the album was 'Walk This Way', which also became the second single, along with the re-release of 'Dream On', to hit the Top 10 of the Billboard Hot 100 in the 1970s. 'Walk This Way' pushed the album even further, making it the most critically acclaimed and commercially successful so far for the band. It rose them up to the top, competing alongside Led Zeppelin and the Rolling Stones, although the similarities were still being noted between the stage presence of Mick Jagger and Steven Tyler. The track often went head to head with 'Sweet Emotion' and 'Dream On' for the title of Aerosmith's signature song. It became one of the band's most important, influential, and recognisable songs; in fact they very rarely omit it from their concert set list, still performing their classic version of the song to this day. And of course, it would resurface again in the 1980s with Run-DMC. The song has also long been a staple of rock radio, garnering regular airplay on mainstream rock, classic rock, and album-oriented rock radio stations. Later, in 2009, it was named one of the greatest hard rock songs of all time by VH1, and it would also be inducted into the Grammy Hall of Fame again in 2019. *Toys in the Attic* would go on in the years ahead to become the band's bestselling studio album in the United States, with certified US sales of eight million copies.

The band immediately toured again in support of *Toys in the Attic*, where they started to get even more recognition. Aerosmith had now made it, and had truly arrived, and the next few years would see them become one of rock's most potent, extreme and celebrated outfits.

It was also around this time that the band established their home base, which they named 'the Wherehouse', situated in Waltham, Massachusetts. This would serve as a permanent base where they could rehearse, record new music and conduct their business affairs. The Wherehouse, which was officially titled A. Wherehouse, was first rented out by Aerosmith in 1975, continuing into the 1980s. The facility featured a garage for the band's various cars and offices upstairs for personnel. On ground level was a full recording studio and a stage for full rehearsals, and the band used the space as a place to hang out, write and relax between tours while they were located in Boston. The Wherehouse was also the birthplace of the official fan club of the band, Aero Force One. Ray Tabano, who had left the band, started up the club in 1971, and he started writing newsletters and selling merchandise out of the building. Tabano was also responsible for the general maintenance of the building and its offices, which would also be rented out to other bands on occasion; for example the band Boston won their own record deal by playing for record executives there when they rented the space.

The tour in support of the album started in March 1975, scheduled for North America, and the band went to the western US for the first time. It was here that their true following started as they were now headlining their own shows completely. The sets changed as the band toured but the basic set list was: 'Walkin' the Dog', 'S.O.S. (Too Bad)', 'Somebody', 'Big Ten Inch Record', 'Sweet Emotion', 'Dream On', 'Write Me a Letter', 'Walk This Way', 'No More No More', 'Same Old Song and Dance', 'The Train Kept A-Rollin'' and 'Toys in the Attic'. The tour ended in San Diego on December 30th at The San Diego Arena.

As 1976 came around Aerosmith turned again to writing and started working on their next album. It was recorded between February and March 1976 at the Wherehouse in Waltham, Massachusetts with the Record Plant Mobile and The Record Plant in New York City. The album showcased the band at their most rocking and raw. It was a period infused by drugs and excess, during which 'the bad boys from Boston' became the living breathing essence of sex, drugs and rock and roll, and no band could match them.

Rocks was released on May 14th 1976, although it was delayed slightly on release for copyright reasons. The album cemented their status as hard rock superstars. They had found a cutting edge within rock and roll and live performance and developed a sort of standard for power ballads, starting with 'Dream On'. Aerosmith's ability to pull off both ballads and rock 'n' roll made them extremely popular, and with *Rocks* their status again grew rapidly worldwide. Following constant touring and their ferocious live shows the band now had a huge loyal following, and furthermore their considerable hedonism and drug fuelled indulgences had no effect on their creativity. *Rocks* for this reason has always been considered by many fans, critics, and fellow musicians to be one of the highlights of their entire career.

The final listing on *Rocks* after the recording sessions was as follows. Side one: 'Back in the Saddle' written by Steven Tyler and Joe Perry, 'Last Child' written by Steven Tyler and Brad Whitford, 'Rats in the Cellar' written by Steven Tyler and Joe

Perry and 'Combination' written by Joe Perry. Side two: 'Sick As a Dog' written by Steven Tyler and Tom Hamilton, 'Nobody's Fault', written by Steven Tyler and Brad Whitford, 'Get the Lead Out' and 'Lick And A Promise' both written by Steven Tyler and Joe Perry and finally 'Home Tonight' written by Steven Tyler. Performing on the album were Steven Tyler on lead vocals, keyboards and harmonica, Joe Perry on guitars and vocals, Brad Whitford also on guitars, Tom Hamilton on bass and additional vocals and Joey Kramer on drums and also providing additional vocals.

The album was correctly named in every way, and even though there was widespread speculation and later acknowledgment of drug use within the band, this escalation still managed to produce an outstanding follow up to the master work that was *Toys in the Attic*. *Toys* was seen by many as the quintessential Aerosmith album, having produced two radio and concert staples in 'Walk This Way' and 'Sweet Emotion', but *Rocks* moved Aerosmith into high octane rocking monsters. It's the perfect follow on from *Toys in the Attic* and brings another progression to the notoriety and reputation of the band as the pure rock machines they were now becoming. Like its predecessor before it, two songs in particular stood out and became renowned in the Aerosmith live canon, these being the menacing hard rocker of 'Back in the Saddle' and the dirty groove of 'Last Child'. The other tracks on the album blended perfectly, ending with the closing ballad 'Home Tonight'.

There comes a time in an artist's or band's evolution when they simply cannot do anything wrong, each release being a step forward and an improvement on the last record, whilst simultaneously complementing it. This is where Aerosmith were with *Rocks*. The band were looking formidable and steadily improved with each release, progressing and developing within the American hard rock market, and the album showcases perfectly an excellent hard rock band at the peak of their powers. Throughout the album is consistently catchy, with memorable riffs, grooves, and arrangements, plenty of swagger and attitude, and Steven Tyler's vocals are also a fabulous highlight, including his underrated harmonies. *Rocks* is a cohesive, compulsive listen and hits hard from the first to the last note. It has the intensity of the music, the larynx-shredding vocals of Steven Tyler, and the continued improvements in the writing, which again is equally shared throughout the band. It makes *Rocks* an album not just to jam to but to appreciate the raw power Aerosmith possessed in these formative years. Here you can see the legacy that Aerosmith would have on later bands: the record influenced 80s and even 90s rock/metal from bands like Guns N' Roses, Nirvana, Soundgarden, Motley Crue and Metallica.

In typical Aerosmith style the band immediately hit the road again. The difference here however was that The Rocks Tour would be the band's first major headlining tour. Beginning in April 1976 the band played some of the largest stadiums in the US, including the Silverdome, the Kingdome, Three Rivers Stadium, Angels Stadium, Sun Devil Stadium, and Comiskey Park. The tour in autumn would also take them across to Europe for the first time, supported by Phoenix, and later on in February 1977 across to Japan, again for the first time. They had many other opening acts during the tour, these including Jeff Beck, Bob Seger, REO Speedwagon, Rush, and Nazareth. The usual set list for the shows comprised of 'Mama Kiln', 'S.O.S. (Too Bad)'/ 'Write Me A Letter', 'Lick And A Promise', 'Big Ten Inch Record', 'Sweet Emotion', 'Rats In The Cellar', 'Dream On', 'Lord of the Thighs', 'Last Child', 'Walk This Way', 'Sick As A Dog', 'Same Old Song And Dance', 'Train Kept A-Rollin', 'Get The Lead Out', 'Toys In The Attic' and 'Nobody's Fault'. The North American leg kicked off the tour, starting at Keil Auditorium in St Louis, and over 60 shows followed from April through to September 1976, including a show in Toronto in July. The European leg kicked off in Liverpool at The Empire on October 13th 1976, and the band then travelled to Glasgow for a show in Scotland before a show in Birmingham at The Odeon; it was then on to London for the final concert in the UK on October 17th at The Hammersmith Odeon. The band then played through Germany, Sweden, the Netherlands, Switzerland and France, which concluded the European leg on November 1st 1976. The band returned again to North America for more shows starting in Pittsburgh on November 10th, and they played a further ten concerts including another in Canada, this time in Montreal at The Forum, before this leg concluded at the Carolina Coliseum on December 19th. The Asia leg of the tour took in a total of seven concerts starting in Maebashi at the Gunma Sports centre on January 29th 1977, and they then played Tokyo at the Nippon Budakan, Nagoya at The Assembly Hall, Fukuoko in Japan, Kyoto Kaikan, Osaka Festival Hall in Osaka, and finally ended the tour in Tokyo at Budakan.

The tour had been an incredible success, not just in financial terms but also for well and truly establishing Aerosmith as a truly global rock band with a loyal following of worldwide fans. The last two albums had lifted them into a classic area, a place only a few rock bands frequented. They were both critically and commercially successful and the reputation they had both on and off the stage was unparalleled. *Rocks* had now gone platinum, and with such a brilliant and successful tour behind them they returned to the studio to work on their next album, to further move forward on the worldwide fame they had now cemented. If they could just stay on the straight and narrow, they could take things forward and achieve great things. The band and everyone around them knew this. They needed to stay focused and away from the excessive behaviour that threatened their very existence. They needed to stay determined, stay hungry. Stay on the line.

Drawing the Line

The band had more or less toured constantly over the past few years. The mammoth Rocks Tour had taken them around the world from April 1976 through to February 1977, and with all the touring the band had done over the previous years, things were now beginning to take their toll. The band entered the studio shortly after the tour had finished to work on another album, in June 1977, which would be their fifth release.

Draw the Line was an album in which the excesses of the band were starting to have an effect; that said, the album still delivers, and delivers well. It proved Aerosmith were still capable, despite the various 'distractions', of delivering another raw and stomping rock album. There were more songs that would be added to future tour sets from the album, with 'Draw the Line' and 'Kings and Queens' becoming additional concert favourites. The album was recorded between June and October 1977 at The Cenacle, which was an abandoned convent outside Armonk New York, with the Record Plant Mobile. It was also recorded at The Record Plant itself in New York City. Three singles were released from the album: 'Draw the Line' itself in October 1977, the aforementioned 'Kings and Queens' in February 1978 and 'Get it Up', also in 1978. After recording the sessions, the band finalised the listing as follows. Side one: 'Draw the Line' written by Steven Tyler and Joe Perry, 'I Wanna Know Why' written by Steven Tyler and Joe Perry, 'Critical Mass' written by Steven Tyler, Tom Hamilton and Jack Douglas, 'Get It Up' written by Steven Tyler and Joe Perry and 'Bright Light Fright' written by Joe Perry. Side two: 'Kings and Queens' written by Steven Tyler, Brad Whitford, Tom Hamilton, Joey Kramer and Jack Douglas, 'The Hand That Feeds' written by Steven Tyler, Brad Whitford, Tom Hamilton, Joey Kramer and Jack Douglas, 'Sight for Sore Eyes' written by Steven Tyler, Joe Perry, Jack Douglas and David Johansen and finally 'Milk Cow Blues' written by Kokomo Arnold.

The album was more of a collaborative effort than previous albums from the band. Steven Tyler, as well as the usual lead vocals, also played harmonica and piano on 'Kings and Queens'. Joe Perry played lead guitar, rhythm guitar and slide guitar, sang backing vocals and provided the lead vocals on 'Bright Light Fright'. Brad Whitford played rhythm guitar and lead guitar on 'Kings and Queens', 'I Wanna Know Why', and 'The Hand That Feeds'. He also played the first solo on 'Milk Cow Blues'. Tom Hamilton as usual played bass on the album with Joey Kramer again on all drums and percussion. There were also guest musicians throughout the album. Stan Bronstein played saxophone on 'I Wanna Know Why' and 'Bright Light Fright', Scott Cushnie added piano on 'I Wanna Know Why' and 'Critical Mass', Karen Lawrence provided backing vocals on 'Get It Up', and Jack Douglas added mandolin on 'Kings and Queens' with the banjo on the track played by Paul Prestopino. Production was again by Jack Douglas with the band itself. The cover art for the album was also interesting and a common sign of a band having made the big time; it was illustrated by Al Hirschfeld and features just simple caricatures of the band with no other detail.

The album is excessive and loud, like the band itself, and is purposely over indulgent. The band were now able to afford anything they wanted in the studio and could stretch to accommodate any extra embellishments they thought would enhance the record. The guitars are somewhat low in the mix and it's evident that there was more thought in the production and creation of the record than in previous albums, which were simply belted out, and it's this that splits some critics in their opinions. At this point Steven Tyler and Joe Perry were fondly referred to as 'the toxic twins' and the album was created with the band in its own creative bubble, their own world as such, making the album less technical in its overall delivery; that said, the album works even through the haze of excess. The sessions that took place at The Cenacle were reported to have been very volatile for the band.

The former place of holy worship was treated to a very different kind of guest, and the scene was one of in-fighting, drugs and various other alleged activities rumoured to be happening at the time. The alleged superfluous drug use and various indulgences twinned with the creative in-fighting naturally filtered onto the album and had a negative effect, essentially pulling out any natural creativity that could otherwise flow. *Draw the Line* therefore has many exceptional tracks but they feel less accessible in comparison with previous albums; they require several listens and the hooks are not instantly catchy as before. It feels vastly different from *Toys in the Attic* and *Rocks* and isn't as polished. The band were also trying to recapture the elements of the blues-based rock of their first album and were consciously working to capture it rather than being spontaneous in the recording. Steven Tyler's vocals are in keeping with the album, dark and growly, and they provide some brilliant moments, and it's evident the band wanted to re-establish the direct back to basics hard rock approach.

On release, the first single, 'Draw the Line', provided another hit for the band commercially. It was released with the B-side 'Chip Away The Stone', which was not included on the album but would surface later on *Gems*, a compilation album mainly of harder tracks that were not released as singles. The track was written by Richie Supa and became another concert favourite for the band. There were some versions also released that featured 'Bright Light Fright' as the B-side.

With the album now out the band once again hit the road for more touring. The Aerosmith Express Tour/Draw The Line Tour began on June 21st 1977 and went through until September. The set list varied during the tour but the main staples performed were 'Back in the Saddle', 'Mama Kin', 'Sick as a Dog', 'Dream On', 'Lick and a Promise', 'S.O.S. (Too Bad)', 'Same Old Song and Dance', 'Lord of the Thighs', 'The Train Kept A-Rollin', 'Sweet Emotion' and 'Walk This Way'.

The Draw The Line Tour was extremely successful for the band, but equally arduous and demanding. They had a variety of opening acts along the way, these including Point Blank, AC/DC, Mahogany Rush, Nazareth, and Ted Nugent. The band sounded incredible on this tour, so much so that most of the recording that

31

featured on *Live!*, released a year later, would come from this tour. This double album was released in October 1978 and also features 'I Ain't Got You' and 'Mother Popcorn', which were taken from a performance in Boston on March 20th 1973. 'Chip Away The Stone' was also released as single from the album. The album was interesting in its production; the band wanted the album to sound bootlegged so they purposely played about with the production, and they also added coffee stains to the rear of the artwork. Some of the tracks were even recorded off air onto a cassette so it would add some hiss to the sound. The album was produced by Jack Douglas, Aerosmith themselves, David Krebs and Steve Leber. During this tour Aerosmith headlined the Texxas Jam '78 Festival on July 1st 1978. This would be another later live release and it was made available on video later, in 1989. The band also headlined Cal Jam II in Ontario, CA and the Day on the Green Festival in Oakland, CA, on October 10th 1977.

During the tour the band started to become affected by the reported drug abuse and the fast-paced life they were leading. It started to have a direct effect on their performances. Both Steven Tyler and Joe Perry were now well and truly established as 'the toxic twins' in connection to their constant indulgences. Steven Tyler himself later claimed he had spent $64 million on drugs; however, Joe Perry disagreed with the number, making the point that if that amount of money was spent, he wouldn't be alive. It did however make a great headline, adding to the reputation of the band.

Continuing with their insatiable appetite for live performances and touring the band continued on. The tour Live! Bootleg Tour saw the band play arenas across North America in the autumn of 1978, playing 43 blistering rock shows. Opening acts were again drafted in for support, including Golden Earring amongst others. The band's reputation was now firmly established and the audiences were equally indulgent, following their rock idols and taking things to excess; in fact there were many incidents during the concerts which forced the band to stop playing. At one concert they actually bailed out 53 fans who were reportedly arrested for smoking pot at the show in Fort Wayne, Indiana on October 3, 1978. Ahead to November 25th in Philadelphia, Steven

Tyler was hit by a glass bottle, which forced the concert to be cancelled while he received treatment.

Taking a break from the tour Aerosmith appeared in a new movie and subsequent soundtrack that was in the making: the *Sgt. Pepper's Lonely Hearts Club Band* movie. They recorded a cover of The Beatles' 'Come Together' for the soundtrack, which would provide another hit for the band. The movie was written as an American musical comedy, and was directed by Michael Schultz and written by Henry Edwards. In the film Aerosmith play a band named 'Future Villain Band' or F.V.B. The narrative is a loosely constructed story about a band as they manoeuvre their way through the music industry. The comedy sees them battling evil forces who attempt to steal their instruments while also corrupting their home town, which was warmly named Heartland. The film is presented in the 'rock opera' genre, with the songs adding a sort of dialogue, assisting the story. The film's soundtrack, released as an accompanying double album, features new versions of songs originally written and performed by the Beatles, which include Aerosmith's version of 'Come Together'. The movie is also connected to two Beatles albums, *Sgt. Pepper's Lonely Hearts Club Band* from 1967 and *Abbey Road* from 1969. The movie covers all the songs from the *Sgt. Pepper* album, the only exceptions being 'Within You, Without You' and 'Lovely Rita', and it also includes nearly all of *Abbey Road*. The movie was loosely adapted from a 1974 Broadway production, *Sgt. Pepper's Lonely Hearts Club Band on the Road*, this production being directed by Tom O'Horgan. Aerosmith scored another hit with the cover of 'Come Together' that was featured on the album; the movie however was a bit of a disaster and received mainly negative reviews.

The band concluded the Live! Bootleg Tour on December 12th 1978 at Kansas Coliseum, after 43 gruelling concerts, a movie appearance and a contribution to a soundtrack. It was time now however to go back to the studio, as the pressure was on the band to record again: put simply the label wanted another hit album. The situation this time however was extremely different from before: the recording process was constantly interrupted, and it was slow, and the band had many issues which affected their productivity. In

33

reality, the band were imploding in on themselves. The constant drug abuse and hedonistic lifestyle they had become accustomed to was now well and truly catching up with them, and it was taking its toll.

The recording of their next album, which would eventually become *Night in the Ruts*, began in the spring of 1979, but right from the start there were constant disagreements and lengthy delays. Steven Tyler had issues consistently with lyrics and vocals, which resulted in the album being delayed as they couldn't finish it in the time that was allocated. The album was originally to be called *Off Your Rocker* and was scheduled for a June release but as things went forward it was clear this was not going to happen; it became a crisis for the band. It was also rumoured at the time that Joe Perry owed the band a significant amount of money. He had built this up for 'room service' while on the road; it was allegedly $80,000, which was a vast amount in 1978. His plan was to pay this back by recording a solo album of his own which he was planning. The band's relationship with producer Jack Douglas was also on the decline; he had recently divorced and the band were very much in favour of his wife, who they all had a good relationship with. There were fractures in the band in all directions from the drugs, the alcohol, the pressure from the label and the personal relationships. The record label itself, Columbia, now stepped in, with the growing issues that the band were dealing with. They felt that sales of *Draw the Line* were weaker than anticipated and so wanted another hit from them. They ramped up the pressure on the band to record the album, to make it a hit album and record it quickly. However, with the constant in-fighting, bad atmosphere and drug fuelled issues it was impossible for the band to function as they had before. The band's manager at the time, David Krebs, admitted that he had lost complete control of them; basically no-one had any control during this period at all, let alone the band itself.

The album therefore was left half-finished and without any vocals. In addition the band had used up the entire budget that was allocated. With the album well and truly on pause the band's management booked them again on tour throughout the summer, to generate income. From April through to July 1979, the band were scheduled in to play major festivals in Los Angeles, Orlando, Toronto, Oakland, and Cleveland. The album's allotted time that was given to produce the album was in keeping with previous albums for Aerosmith; this time however they needed a lot longer to get it completed. The record was paused and it dragged on and on as they toured once more. The whole band was extremely frustrated and the substance abuse got worse; the band now were well and truly fighting amongst themselves. The irony was that on tour they were selling out huge festivals and looked like a true rock and roll band; there were some issues as expected with some of the performances but nevertheless they were selling out festivals and drawing in the crowds. Behind the scenes however they were tearing themselves apart. The issues with some of the performances were of course a result of the immense fusion of cocktails the band were consuming. There was one trigger however that finally broke things completely. During the festival tour backstage another argument developed but this time things came to an ugly finale that reportedly involved some of the band's wives. This was the final straw for Joe Perry when, on July 28th 1979, at the World Series of Rock in Cleveland, Ohio, he quit the band after a large argument with Steven Tyler. This was literally half way through the tour.

The last session that Joe Perry played with the band before his departure was on May 30th 1979. As the album was in limbo from April onwards he felt that he had done what he could; he had laid down several guitar parts and he felt that the band could either use it or erase it: his mind at this point had moved on and he was working on his own projects. Despite leaving the band, musically Joe Perry was very happy with what had been put down, and he felt the interplay between himself and Brad Whitford had been superb; he even went as far as to say that he thought it broke new ground. His frustrations however lay with the recording of the vocals and the ongoing problems with Steven Tyler. Joe stated at this point things slowly started to derail and come to a standstill; he was annoyed and felt the band had squandered millions of dollars on hotel bills and studio time and had nothing to show for it. It was alleged also that when Steven Tyler came to do his vocals, he walked in smoking crack, hence the issues with the recording.

Joe Perry wanted simply to play rock and roll at this point and didn't mind if he was driving around in a van and playing small clubs; in his own words, he was tired of the bullshit. The album therefore when it was finally recorded featured only certain guitar parts by Joe Perry, which would essentially be the parts he laid down before he departed the band. These were on 'No Surprize', 'Chiquita', 'Cheese Cake', 'Three Mile Smile' and 'Bone to Bone (Coney Island White Fish Boy)'. The remaining guitar parts were added after and recorded by Brad Whitford, Richie Supa, Neil Thompson and Jimmy Crespo.

Auditions now took place for Joe Perry's replacement, and of course the label wanted this done quickly to get the band back to full strength. The band's long time writing partner Richie Supa stepped in temporarily while the new member was selected. He had previously contributed to 'Chip Away The Stone' in 1978 and later to many more including 'Lightning Strikes' in 1982, 'Amazing' in 1993 and 'Pink' in 1997, among many others. He also would contribute going forward to many hits for Bon Jovi. The album was still required to be completed despite the internal issues and excesses. Jimmy Crespo was at the forefront of the management's radar as a replacement. He had departed his own band, Flame, which had broken up, and had recently returned to session work. He was subsequently invited to audition for the band and was asked to join in October 1979, contributing to a guitar solo on 'Three Mile Smile' as progress on the now renamed *Night in the Ruts* album continued.

Although the band had their new guitarist things were still not as they should be. Jimmy Crespo immediately joined the band as they continued touring but Steven Tyler's state was becoming increasingly erratic. He was now heavily into drug addiction and suffered several live on-stage collapses. With Joe Perry now out of the once formidable unit, drummer Joey Kramer also became frustrated and decided he also would look at moving on. He formed a band called Renegade during this time. He recruited Marge Raymond to sing lead and front the band. Renegade recorded several tracks in SIR Studios in New York City and also Power Station in New York. They went so far at one point as to actually get a record deal, but Tom Hamilton and Joey Kramer were still obligated to Aerosmith for the next album, which would become *Rock in a Hard Place*, so the project they were now putting together never actually materialised as they thought it would. Renegade consisted of Tom Hamilton on bass, Joey Kramer on drums, Jimmy Crespo on lead guitar, Bobby Mayo on rhythm guitar, and Marge Raymond on vocals. Marge had been the lead singer of Jimmy Crespo's former band Flame. The project was put together by Joey Kramer for one simple reason: he could see at this point that Aerosmith was ready to self-destruct. The tracks the band recorded were highly sought after and the non-release actually made it very collectable and a sort of legendary album for fans.

Joe Perry had now formed his own band, The Joe Perry Project, as Aerosmith still worked through the remains of *Night in the Ruts* and their ongoing issues with drug addiction and erratic performances. In 1979 The Joe Perry Project signed almost immediately with Columbia Records, who were increasingly frustrated with the delay of *Night in the Ruts* and Aerosmith's performances. Joe Perry himself was obviously familiar with the label but the label was looking forward as well. They could see that this could eventually bring Perry back to Aerosmith when the in-fighting and substance abuse had worked its way through, maybe. By having both bands on the label it would be easier to bring the circle back around at some point. The band consisted of Joe Perry on guitar, David Hull (who would act as a substitute tour bass player later on for Aerosmith during three world tours) on bass, Hagen Grohe on vocals, Paul Santo on keyboards and guitars and Marty Richards on drums. The band recorded their debut album, *Let the Music Do The Talking*, throughout the remainder of 1979 at the hit factory in New York, as Aerosmith, with the replacement line-ups, simultaneously finished *Night in the Ruts*. *Let the Music Do the Talking* was released a year later in 1980 and the band played in smaller locations in and around the Boston area. The album was renowned as a great album and often overlooked; it was a statement by Joe Perry at the time, in which he went back to his roots and wanted to get away from the politics of the music industry. He wanted to deliver an album that was without a timetable or any kind of external restriction. Ironically many believe the album could have been a classic Aerosmith album if the drug abuse hadn't been tearing the band apart at the time. Therefore, the album remained vastly overlooked and creatively underrated.

The new line up of Aerosmith, with the filling-in musicians, now finally managed to complete their long overdue album. It would be Aerosmith's sixth studio release. The making of it had literally ripped them apart, with key members now branching out into solo projects. *Night in the Ruts* was eventually released in November 1979, but this wasn't in any way a turning point. Things were still on a slippery slope for Steven Tyler and to compound things further the band were quickly booked in to tour again to support the album. Aerosmith were now a band literally hanging on to stay as a cohesive unit in a very competitive area of rock and roll. After the arguments, the breakups, the spending, the hedonistic excess, the alcohol and drugs abuse, if the band didn't last much longer it would literally come as 'No Surprize'.

Stuck Between

Night in The Ruts used the original session work which included Joe Perry, with other musicians stepping in to assist in getting the album completed. The completed tracks were listed as follows. Side one: 'No Surprize' written by Steven Tyler and Joe Perry, 'Chiquita' written by Steven Tyler and Joe Perry, 'Remember (Walking in the Sand)' (The Shangri-Las cover) written by Shadow Morton, and 'Cheese Cake' written by Steven Tyler and Joe Perry. Side two started with 'Three Mile Smile' written by Steven Tyler and Joe Perry, then 'Reefer Head Woman' (Jazz Gillum cover) written by Joe Bennett, Jazz Gillum and Lester Melrose, 'Bone to Bone (Coney Island White Fish Boy)' written by Steven Tyler and Joe Perry, 'Think About It' (The Yardbirds cover) written by Keith Relf, Jimmy Page and Jim McCarty, and the final track 'Mia' written by Steven Tyler.

The album was produced by Gary Lyons who, despite the state of the band at the time, managed to get the album through to completion at Media Sound in New York. Steven Tyler, although having many issues, managed to get some inspiration when he wrote the lyrics for 'No Surprize', which had originally been left unfinished. It told the story of the band, and he said it was his favourite track, and it's this that moved the album forward very quickly once it was completed. 'No Surprize' was the track that turned Steven Tyler back on form: he had admitted to having a complete block but this was satisfying for him, and he was excited that it came together and gave him hope that through the problems he could still turn out a quality rock song in the Aerosmith sound. On 'Reefer Head Woman', which was a blues record from the 1940s, Steven had the lyrics stolen from a notebook he had, so the lyrics were later read to him over the phone so he could complete the track. The song 'Mia' was written by Steven Tyler for his daughter; however many who knew the band at the time felt that the bell notes at the end of the track were there to signify the end of the band. 'Mia' was also the last track on the album, so a fitting close. The was a bit of confusion over the track 'Bone to Bone (Coney Island White Fish Boy)': Steven had to explain afterwards that a Coney Island whitefish is a used condom notoriously found on Coney Island beach. The album featured covers, which is unsurprising considering what was going on within the band; 'Think About It' was a Yardbirds song and actually a B-side from 1968. Aerosmith liked the song and had played it several times while touring.

Despite all that was going on in and around the band, Steven Tyler was very excited about *Night in the Ruts* and went so far as to call it his favourite album. He claimed later that it involved heroin, shooting coke and eating opium and it felt like a complete 'solar eclipse'. Joe Perry also enjoyed the finished product, saying he felt it was a real rocking record and more cohesive in sound than the previous *Draw the Line*. It's a more blues-based sound, leaner, and an attempt to return to the core foundations of the band. The critics however were less than complimentary and, on the whole, didn't favour it alongside the previous albums. It was clear that many felt that the band, now without its core members, were on the way down and destined to end. The album also suffered because of the incomplete nature it was left in; it lost its spontaneous nature, which produced some of Aerosmith's greatest work.

There was huge list of collaborators on the finished record outside of the normal core band. Standard members gave the usual contribution: Steven Tyler on lead vocals, keyboards, harmonica and piano with Joe Perry adding guitar, slide guitar and backing vocals on 'No Surprize', 'Chiquita', 'Cheese Cake', 'Three Mile Smile', and 'Bone to Bone (Coney Island White Fish Boy)' before his departure. Brad Whitford also played guitar with Tom Hamilton on bass and Joey Kramer on drums. Additional musicians who were drafted in were Mary Weiss on backing vocals on 'Remember (Walking in the Sand)', Richie Supa drafted in to add additional guitars on 'No Surprize' and 'Mia' and Jimmy Crespo adding his lead guitar on 'Three Mile Smile' before getting the nod as a replacement for Joe Perry. Louis del Gatto added baritone saxophone, Lou Marini added tenor saxophone, Barry Rogers added trombone, Neil Thompson added guitar and George Young added alto saxophone, all on 'Chiquita'. Alongside producer Gary Lyons was David Krebs who acted as executive producer.

Night in the Ruts performed reasonably well at the time and it peaked at number 14. It was certified gold. While the album performed respectably on the charts, the ensuing tour did little to boost sales; it didn't help either that the tour was marred with cancelled dates and the sometimes lacklustre performances brought on by Tyler's substance abuse. Unsurprisingly it was the least successful Aerosmith record to date. It would of course have a massive resurgence when the band once again hit the top of the charts years later and became one of the biggest rock bands on the planet. Any band with longevity will always enjoy their back catalogue becoming sought after and admired, even if at the time of the release it was not what they initially expected it to be, or it was not fully appreciated. Nostalgia for past albums is a wonderful thing.

The tour that followed the album was focused on North America; it was the first tour to feature new guitarist Jimmy Crespo, who had now officially replaced Joe Perry. It ran from July 1979 through to December 1980 and loosely followed the following set list: 'The Train Kept A-Rollin', 'S.O.S. (Too Bad)', 'Mama Kin', 'Reefer Head Woman', 'Lick and a Promise', 'Think About It', 'Seasons of Wither', 'Bone to Bone (Coney Island White Fish Boy)', 'Lord of the Thighs', 'Sweet Emotion', 'Get the Lead Out' and 'Walk This Way'. What was significant however was the band were now playing much smaller venues than previously. The new the line-up of Jimmy Crespo replacing Joe Perry and Rock Dufay replacing Brad Whitford for some just didn't feel the same, and in addition Steven Tyler was now reaching rock bottom and his performances were suffering. He had many high profile on-stage collapses during this period. The band now settled back in, determined to record another album and win

41

back their popularity once more. Steven Tyler however was still suffering from various excesses and this would continue through the writing and recording of their next venture, *Rock in a Hard Place*. It would be the band's seventh studio album.

During the recording of one of the tracks on the album, 'Lightning Strikes', Brad Whitford finally left the band, forming the Whitford/St. Holmes Band with former Ted Nugent guitarist Derek St. Holmes. A year later in 1981, they recorded their self-titled first album. The album was followed by a tour but the album and the tour to promote it failed to be successful. As a result, in 1983, Whitford reunited with Joe Perry to play live at several shows with his band The Joe Perry Project before they both went full circle and reunited with Aerosmith.

Brad Whitford was quickly replaced by Rick Dufay, who now also replaced him full time on the tour circuit. Steven Tyler's addiction was now significant and he was allegedly walking the streets looking for dealers to feed his ongoing habits. In addition, and to add further to his troubles, he suffered a serious motorcycle crash in the autumn of 1980 in which he was badly injured. The injuries he sustained left him hospitalised for two months, which of course left him unable to record much; it also meant that he couldn't tour and he spent most of 1981 recovering from his injuries. When the band finally settled back into the recording Steven Tyler began a creative partnership with Jimmy Crespo and the pair started writing and bouncing ideas off each other. The results of this new partnership led to Jimmy Crespo co-writing six of the tracks and contributing to most of the guitar parts on *Rock in a Hard Place*. The album was recorded at The Power Station in New York City and Criteria Studios in Miami.

The expense of the new album was considerable and the band threw everything at it. It was reported that the record cost between $1 and $2 million in production costs alone, a vast amount in 1981/82, and it featured a growing list of collaborators in production and engineering staff including Jack Douglas, who they were now reacquainted with. The final track listing after the recording sessions took place was finalised as follows. Side one: 'Jailbait' written by Steven Tyler and Jimmy Crespo, 'Lightning Strikes' written by Steven Tyler, Jimmy Crespo and Richard Supa,

'Bitch's Brew' written by Steven Tyler and Jimmy Crespo, 'Bolivian Ragamuffin' written by Steven Tyler and Crespo and 'Cry Me a River' written by Arthur Hamilton. Side two: 'Prelude to Joanie' written by Steven Tyler, 'Joanie's Butterfly' written by Steven Tyler, Jimmy Crespo, and Jack Douglas, 'Rock in a Hard Place (Cheshire Cat)' written by Steven Tyler, Jimmy Crespo and Jack Douglas, 'Jig Is Up' written by Steven Tyler and Jimmy Crespo and 'Push Comes to Shove' written by Steven Tyler. Steven Tyler played his usual contributions to the album: lead vocals, keyboards, harmonica, percussion and piano on 'Push Comes to Shove'. Jimmy Crespo played lead guitar, sang backing vocals, and also added additional vocals on 'Bitch's Brew'. Tom Hamilton played bass on the album with Joey Kramer on drums. Rick Dufay was credited on the album for rhythm guitar but it was rumoured that he didn't actually play. The additional musicians outside the main band were Paul Harris who also played piano on 'Push Comes to Shove', John Turi playing saxophone on 'Rock in a Hard Place (Cheshire Cat)', Reinhard Straub contributing violin on 'Joanie's Butterfly' and John Lievano on acoustic guitar, also on 'Joanie's Butterfly'. Jack Douglas added percussion as well as production.

The album was released in August 1982, again on Colombia Records. Two singles were scheduled for release: 'Lightning Strikes' and 'Bitch's Brew'. 'Lightning Strikes' was released as a promotional single to rock radio, and it reached 21 on the US Mainstream Rock Tracks Chart. What was also significant for the single was a huge sea change happening within the music industry. It was a change that the band would benefit from enormously in the next few years. Until this point record sales were relatively simple to calculate; they were recorded as the amount of sales an album or single sold, in the physical sense, through shops. Bands released singles and would put together a music video that would hopefully get some airplay on TV. In promoting these new albums and to boost sales further acts like Aerosmith would hit the road, playing live and drawing attention to their album, building along the way a huge fan base. An artist or band had to work to get promotion: there was no Internet, no Facebook, no Twitter or Instagram. There was however a new promotional tool taking hold

43

at this time and, if you could get it right, the rewards from getting noticed and capturing new fans could be massive. It was taking the music world by storm, growing every day, and the industry realised that to get instant worldwide exposure it was this new trend that a band or artist needed to be part of.

The medium of the music video was growing and it was growing fast: it was becoming an essential part of promotion for any band. Before it was seen as an add-on, an extra piece of promotion for singles. Now it was becoming an almost essential part of the promotional and marketing budget for bands. Seeing this growth, the music video market gave birth to a dedicated channel and saw the introduction of Music Television, or, as it would soon be known around the world, MTV. Aerosmith with 'Lightning Strikes' created one of their earliest actual music videos for MTV and other networks. It was directed by Arnold Levine and runs back and forth between the band performing in what appears to be a studio or small venue and then out on the streets. The band look angry and wield baseball bats, chains, knives, and other weapons, suggesting a fight is about to take place. The song also features fake lightning strikes during the transitions between the band's performance and the streets, with baseball bats striking melons in the air. It was a great early promotion that fitted the MTV movement, and gave the band some early exposure as MTV grew more popular.

MTV itself was a joint venture between American Express and Warner Communications. It made its first appearance in August 1981 but by 1983 it had an audience of around 15 million and was growing rapidly. Music videos were becoming a vital part of any artist's repertoire and now an essential part of promotion. MTV targeted the mid 20s generation who were being abandoned by radio stations, and it was, until this point, a rock and roll medium leaning toward white acts. Black artists were very much the minority, particularly for MTV. A major crossover around this time took place when forward thinking and revolutionary artists such as Prince had their songs added. This opened up the genre and gave what would traditionally be a separate market, ie the Black chart, equal running with white acts. At this point charts included Black Music charts and they were separate, but now artists such as

Prince, who had a huge crossover appeal, instantly had their music videos added to the everyday playlists on MTV. This soon paved the way the way for Whitney Houston, Lionel Richie, Tina Turner and Janet Jackson, which kept this crossover going. This crossover held its own until mainstream rap acts emerged in the mid to late 80s and became a regular feature for black artists, and of course Run-DMC with Aerosmith would soon capitalise on this crossover even more. The small but important intervention by MTV was in 1982 when it added the videos for Prince from his album *1999* to its playlist: 'Little Red Corvette' and the title track '1999' itself. Artists like Prince, Whitney Houston and others became mainstream even though before this exposure they were seen as predominantly black music artists. MTV helped blur the edges of what were once separate categories of music. White, black, rock and pop all became intertwined together. It added a new audience and opened up a significant amount of exposure that an artist or band would not ordinarily have had. Without this it is fair to say it may have taken years of continuous touring to reach the same level of exposure; the albums that had singles on the MTV playlist started to accelerate up the charts, and audiences grew rapidly. Record companies were now not just categorising artists on appearance, black, white, rock or pop, but were looking at whether they had someone with the potential to cross over to the mainstream. What was before a relatively underground act, or an act within a certain genre, could now easily reach a huge audience almost overnight.

Rock in a Hard Place gathered mixed reviews from fans, and continued to do so in the years ahead, with many feeling it was the end of Aerosmith altogether. This was in the main due to the absence of Aerosmith's two former and most recognised guitarists; this was the first album on which Joe Perry and Brad Whitford didn't appear. Even before, on previous recordings when they had exited the band, their past work was used, but here for the first time they were completely absent. Many felt that the two new members just didn't possess the quality of either Brad Whitford or Joe Perry, or fans just didn't like the fact that they were not there; a certain dynamic, a familiarity, was missing.

That said, the album taken on its own merit has significant highlights, notably 'Lightning Strikes', 'Bolivian Ragamuffin', 'Joanie's Butterfly' and 'Push Comes to Shove'. It was widely considered that lyrically the album was under par and that the vocals were substandard compared to previous Aerosmith albums, which under the circumstances around this time would be understandable. The classic Aerosmith sound that dominated much of the 1970s was still in here; however, the times were changing and they needed to evolve. The album was, however, despite some negativity in comparison to *Toys in the Attic* or *Rocks*, extremely enjoyable.

Aerosmith here were at rock bottom, and the drug abuse and excess of Steven Tyler over the past few years showed no sign of slowing down. It was insanely remarkable that despite all of this the band still managed to release albums that were in the main better than most of the competition around them. The performances also still continued and the tour around *Rock in a Hard Place* took them all the way through 1984. They were still playing smaller venues however, and Steven Tyler still struggled some nights to stay on his feet, in true rock and roll legend style. The tour continued regardless as before with Jimmy Crespo and Rick Dufay on guitars; however, things were about to change.

The last stop in the tour was in Providence on February 17, 1984. It was during this homecoming concert that a significant change re-established itself for the band. This concert was attended by both Joe Perry and Brad Whitford. Joe Perry had recently divorced and his solo band was coming to an end. They began talks about reuniting the original members and the talks went well. Joe Perry and Brad Whitford now started to be integrated back into the band. Even though years had passed, the second they got back together there was a buzz, and they knew they had made the right move. It would be regarded as one of the most remarkable comeback stories in rock and roll history. They were Back in the Saddle.

Back to Stay, Back in the Saddle

The band, although now fully reenergised, didn't have any new material written. What they had though was an appetite to tour and to show fans they were back, and back with a vengeance. Joe Perry was now coming out of his heroin addiction and Steven Perry was also starting to get himself straightened up. Alcohol however was still around and they were far from clean living: this was still 'the toxic twins' after all. They both now acknowledged that although they had more or less hated each other over the past few years, time was a great healer. They both knew, and had proved, that they needed each other. As a unit, the band's original members were the strength, the core. It was this that *was* Aerosmith, and here on this tour they would set about making this the case for all to see.

The tour started on June 22nd 1984 in Concord at the Capitol Theatre and over the next few months would re-establish the band as one of the most formidable rock bands on the planet. The set list covered the band's career, with many concert favourites now added. The set list roughly followed the following: 'Rats In The Cellar', 'Back In The Saddle', 'Bone To Bone (Coney Island White Fish Boy)', 'Big Ten Inch Record', 'Movin' Out', 'Last Child', 'Let The Music Do The Talking' (sometimes this would be the Joe Perry Project version), 'Red House' (The Jimi Hendrix Experience cover), 'Dream On', 'Sweet Emotion', 'Same Old Song And Dance'. The band, depending on the venue, would come on for an encore which consisted of 'Walk This Way' and 'Train Kept A-Rollin'. The first leg covered 35 dates with each and every one gaining increased attention for the reunited band. The last concert of the first leg was in Oakland at the County Coliseum Arena on August 31st. After a short break the tour recommenced on December 3rd and took them through until mid-January 1985. At the New Year's Eve concert at the Orpheum Theatre in Boston six tracks were recorded that would eventually feature on *Classics Live II*, which would be a major collectable album for rock fans going forward. The final concert was in Columbus Ohio at Battelle Hall on January 18th. The tour was heralded as a major success in every single way. As the band were now re-forming, they didn't have any current record deal, and a tour could rectify this. As a result, they were not only establishing themselves again to the fans but also advertising themselves again as a band to be signed. It was a huge gamble as they set off on tour with no deal. They considered doing as many as 70 performances; the final results however were just as impressive, as they played 58 concerts in total.

The gamble paid off on the strength of the band as a live offering. They drew the interest of Geffen Records, which eventually led the band to sign a new deal with them. The former label Columbia however still benefitted from live albums and compilations featuring past tracks. *Classics Live!* is made up of concert recordings from 1978 and 1984 while *Gems*, released later in 1988, featured tracks recorded from 1972 through to 1982. The tour gave the band incredible kudos in the live arena and established them once more as a live band of incredible stature. The fans loved them: here they had the balance right between the excess and hard living of a rock band but without the drug and alcohol fuelled chaos disrupting the performances. It was of course still pandemonium, with problems still surfacing during performances and backstage, but they were no longer in 'complete' disarray. There was for the first time in years an organised element to the mayhem, and it's this that worked perfectly for Aerosmith. The tour also gave them financial success, with a reported $3 million in revenue from the tour, the equivalent of around $7 million today. The Back in the Saddle Tour was hugely significant for Aerosmith and was a major turning point in the history, longevity and success of the band going forward. This comeback tour re-established Aerosmith completely. From the end of The Back in the Saddle Tour, they literally never looked back.

Smoke & Mirrors

The band were now back as the original members: Steven Tyler, Joe Perry, Brad Whitford, Tom Hamilton and Joey Kramer. They had just completed a hugely successful comeback tour and had signed a new deal with Geffen Records. It was time now to head to the studio to record once more. In early 1985 the band recorded tracks at Fantasy Studios in Berkeley, California, The Power Station in New York City and Can-Am Recorders in California. The results of these sessions would be *Done with Mirrors,* the band's eighth studio album. The first single scheduled for release from the album was 'Let the Music Do the Talking' which was a rerecording of the title track from the first album by the Joe Perry Project. This new version came with altered lyrics and a slightly changed melody. The final listing was scheduled as follows. Side one: 'Let the Music Do the Talking' written by Steven Tyler and Joe Perry, 'My Fist Your Face' written by Steven Tyler and Joe Perry, 'Shame on You' written by Steven Tyler and 'The Reason a Dog' written by Steven Tyler and Tom Hamilton. Side two: 'Shela' written by Steven Tyler and Brad Whitford, 'Gypsy Boots' written by Steven Tyler and Joe Perry, 'She's on Fire' written by Steven Tyler and Joe Perry and 'The Hop' written by Steven Tyler, Tom Hamilton, Joey Kramer, Joe Perry and Brad Whitford. The CD and cassette came with the bonus track 'Darkness' written by Steven Tyler. There was a 12" vinyl release a year later that featured 'Darkness', which was taken from a concert in Massachusetts on March 12 1986. Other tracks on the 12" included 'She's on Fire', 'The Hop' and 'My Fist Your Face', which were all live recordings taken from this concert.

Done with Mirrors was produced by Ted Templeman, who purposely tried to keep the boys away from their standard 'off the record practices and distractions'. He also used a technique to capture the pure rawness of the band. He recorded them without them knowing they were being recorded. Instead of the red light coming on and the band playing certain parts he opted instead to get them to play spontaneously, running through various songs as if they were playing live, and he then recorded them without any light being shown. He had previously tried this with Van Halen and felt it added a certain aggression to the songs that could disappear once they had a controlled 'cue' and a red light to record.

The cover for the album had all the text back to front, except the catalogue number, so as to be read when holding it up to a mirror. All the text in the booklet of the first CD that was released also had text back to front. The original CD had the artwork flipped in various ways so became very collectable. The title was said to reference illusions that are 'done with mirrors', but it also represented cocaine use, which was traditionally snorted off a mirror. As well as 'Let the Music Do the Talking', which was released in September 1985, 'Shela', 'My Fist Your Face' and 'Darkness' were also drafted in as singles. 'Shela' was released in October with 'My Fist Your Face' and 'Darkness' as US Promos. 'Darkness' was also released as the aforementioned 12" vinyl with accompanying live tracks. Although 'Let the Music Do the Talking' was the first track from the album to be released to radio stations in the US as a promo single it was actually the second single, 'Shela', that was the album's first commercially released single. It reached number 20 on Billboard's Mainstream Rock Tracks Chart towards the end of 1985. The band decided not to release a music video for it.

There's an aggression to the lyrical side of *Done with Mirrors* that showcased the comeback the band wanted to portray. The subjects are dark and reference drug use, underage drug use, sex, underage prostitution and prison sex amongst other similar subject matter. Joe Perry on release of the album was not complimentary about it. He has said on more than one occasion that it was his least favourite album. Critics at the time were also contemptuous towards it and at the time didn't send much praise

50

its way. The feeling was that, despite the comeback and successful Back in the Saddle Tour, Aerosmith were burnt out and devoid of ideas. The album in its original vinyl form only had the eight tracks and ran for just 36 minutes. It was in essence a short album, more in feeling towards an in-between EP as opposed to a structured album. It was for the band an album to release before the next one, which would return them to the top once again. For now, the album hit the edge of the charts, at number 36, and quickly sank down. Once the next albums came along, *Permanent Vacation* in 1987 and then *Pump* in 1989, *Done with Mirrors* disappeared completely from the radar. That said, many hard-core fans however still favoured it, seeing it as a significant step forward to returning the band to the top of the rock world, the first album recorded after the comeback tour and the first album when the band finally got back together. Of course, with all albums time is a great healer and on reflection it faired better than it did when it landed at the time; it is seen therefore as a 'pivotal' album in the back catalogue of Aerosmith. They were down, looking up, and fighting once more for something to cling to, something that would start the rise back from the gutter. The rawness and edge were there, it was volatile, and it felt that the band from here could either go one way or the other: they were literally on the edge. It was an album that ended the 70s cocktail of drugs and alcohol and sent them forward into cleaning themselves up, producing albums that would go multiplatinum throughout the late 1980s and 1990s. It was a catalyst for change in the band's fortunes.

Despite the album's lack of immediate success, one thing that Aerosmith always had was the live attraction. They were simply a brilliant live rock band. Now, as the earlier Back in the Saddle Tour had proved, they didn't need to hesitate to get back out there in support of their new album. The Done with Mirrors Tour lasted an entire year: it actually began before the release itself and went right through to the summer of 1986. It was also during this tour that a significant change in the band's fortunes would emerge. Throughout August and September 1985, they played some warm up shows in areas where the band had a strong following; this was also to promote the forthcoming album before it was eventually released in November. The main tour itself

51

started in January 1986 playing in arenas through to August in the US. The set list followed the standard Aerosmith staples at the time mixed in with the new tracks from *Done with Mirrors*. The concerts started with 'Back in the Saddle', then 'Same Old Song and Dance', 'Bone To Bone (Coney Island White Fish Boy)', 'Big Ten Inch Record', 'My Fist Your Face', 'Last Child', 'No Surprize', 'She's On Fire', 'The Hop', 'Lightning Strikes', 'Shela', 'Walk This Way', 'Let the Music Do the Talking', 'Sweet Emotion', 'Toys in the Attic', 'Dream On', 'Train Kept A-Rollin' and 'Rats in the Cellar'. The band's support were Divinyls at the beginning with Ted Nugent taking over the support for the rest of the scheduled dates. The tour was successful and they performed in large stadiums, and in strong areas such as Massachusetts they would have to perform an extra night to meet demand. The commercial success of the album however was a disappointment and as the tour progressed it fell from the charts. The band, although being an incredible live draw, were in need of chart success, and in need bad: they simply couldn't continue as just a live act alone. It was here that things turned.

Ironically, 'Walk This Way' was sandwiched in the middle of the set list for the Done with Mirrors Tour; however, there was a band from a completely different area of music - one that in 1986 you could say was a completely different world altogether - that was paying attention to the track.

With just a month or so left until the end of the tour Steven Tyler and Joe Perry were contacted as hip-hop band Run-DMC were looking at covering 'Walk This Way', the original recording from 1975. Run-DMC were founded in Queens, New York, in 1981 by Joseph Simmons, Darryl McDaniels, and Jason Mizell. This would be the start of a journey for the band into the mainstream, bringing hip-hop across to the masses. They would go on to be one of the most influential acts in the history of hip-hop culture, and certainly one of the most famous hip-hop acts of the 1980s. The band went into the studio in 1986 working with Def Jam founder Rick Rubin, who would be the producer for this album in the making, which would be their third album *Raising Hell*. They had been freestyling over the track for a while and even used it in live sets they were performing around this time. Rick Rubin had recently produced LL Cool J's debut album *Radio* and was working with Run-DMC on *Raising Hell* with the album nearly completed and ready for release. Rubin wanted to marry together hip-hop and rock, and create something that would appeal to both genres. MTV at this point was growing fast and the crossover of black artists through to mainstream was happening quickly. Black artists were no longer being pigeonholed into 'Black' charts per se but were now becoming integrated very quickly into the mainstream Billboard chart system. There was also a fusion in styles coming through and the boundaries and segregation that were once in music were starting to unravel. Hip-hop especially blurred the edges as it was sampling from other areas of music. Dance also used this technology; music was changing and changing quickly.

Originally the band were just going to rap over a sample of the track but Rubin wanted it as a complete cover version. He played them *Toys in the Attic* and explained to them who Aerosmith were. Steven Tyler and Joe Perry were called to join Run-DMC and they agreed to add vocals and lead guitar respectively. Run-DMC didn't want the record to be released as a single even after recording with Aerosmith members and were shocked when it was played all over the radio, on both urban and rock stations. The single became a huge success on the Billboard Hot 100, reaching number four. It was however bigger than the chart position represented: it was a significant milestone for hip-hop, pushing it forward into mainstream music and indeed culture. In the UK it gave Aerosmith a huge following; until this point, mainly because of distribution, the band's albums were not readily available in the UK. Both Run-DMC and Aerosmith now had a major piece of exposure and the song worked perfectly.

The video helped the track even more, putting the rock band in a room next door to the hip-hop band at the start so they are separated only to break through and bring it all together towards the end. It was symbolic in its message but it worked. The video then segues to the bands' joint performance on stage. It was a hybrid of a video as such and was played in heavy rotation on MTV at the time. It was directed by Jon Small and filmed at the Park Theatre in Union City, New Jersey. Jon Small had previously directed Whitney Houston's 'The Greatest Love of All' and it was thought that here he could get another black act to crossover to the mainstream. He had the idea of featuring Steven Tyler and Joe Perry and thought that they needed to be included for it to work properly. None of the other band members in the video are Aerosmith members. It was reported that this would have been too expensive. Steven Tyler was hesitant about appearing in the video; he was nervous that it might be mocking the band. There was also minimal interaction between the bands at the start of the shoot, although it did open up as it went along. For Run-DMC they went on to shape popular culture through hip-hop alongside many others on this wave of popularity. The single 'My Adidas' led to the group signing a $1,600,000 endorsement deal with athletic apparel brand Adidas. Adidas formed a long-term relationship with Run-DMC and indeed hip-hop. The success of *Raising Hell* is often credited with kick-starting hip-hop's golden age. It gave it a huge visibility and made it a commercial viability. It was now on the international stage and became a global movement of its own in both music and popular culture. 'Walk This Way' went on to become one of the biggest hits of the 1980s; it managed a perfect crossover for both bands and for Aerosmith it well and truly resurrected their career. They now could start to concentrate on fully cleaning themselves up and producing a polished hit album on the back of their newfound success and notoriety. It literally brought the band to a new generation. From here onwards they never looked back. From here on the success was Permanent.

Permanent Return

Aerosmith were now poised and in a good place. There were still issues however that needed to be sorted out within the band. In 1986 Steven Tyler agreed to and completed a successful drug rehabilitation program. It was a group intervention by the band members, a doctor and the group's manager Tim Collins that persuaded Steven to undertake the programme. Many felt that if he didn't do it now it could signal the end of the band, or indeed himself. The rest of the band followed suit and over the next 12-18 months enrolled on similar rehabilitation courses in a bid to get clean. In 1986 Tim Collins had stated that he could make Aerosmith the biggest band in the world in four years if they all completed drug rehab. They agreed, entered rehab and worked solidly to make the next album a success.

The band settled into Little Mountain Sound Studios between March and May 1987 located in Vancouver, Canada. For the first time they worked with external songwriters as well as the band itself to add some input into the songs and initial ideas. They also worked with producer Bruce Fairbairn who had previously produced the multi-platinum *Slippery When Wet* by Bon Jovi. Bruce Fairbairn and Bob Rock used the studios frequently as their favoured place for producing records and it's easy to understand why. During the 1970s, 1980s, and 1990s the studio became the most successful recording studio in Western Canada. For rock bands around this time it was a place of success and would continue to be so going forward. Little Mountain recorded albums for many others selling multi-platinum albums as well as Aerosmith. These included Bon Jovi, AC/DC, Metallica, Bryan

Adams, Mötley Crüe, David Lee Roth, Loverboy and The Cult amongst many others. During the the mid-1990s Little Mountain would eventually become part of Vancouver Studios before it evolved into Greenhouse Studios where it would record albums by Nickelback, k.d. Lang, Default and Queensrÿche. Aerosmith settled in and started working with their new producer and songwriters through several songs, the result of which would be *Permanent Vacation,* their ninth studio album, released in August of this year. The album was a complete success for the band and achieved everything they wanted at the time. It was a concise highly polished rock album and it fitted the band and the charts perfectly following on from the exposure and chart success of 'Walk This Way'; it was for Aerosmith the perfect record at the perfect time. It was a complete turning point in their career.

The final track listing after the sessions was 'Heart's Done Time' written by Steven Tyler, Joe Perry and Desmond Child, 'Magic Touch' written by Steven Tyler, Joe Perry and Jim Vallance, 'Rag Doll' written by Steven Tyler, Joe Perry, Jim Vallance and Holly Knight, 'Simoriah' written by Steven Tyler, Joe Perry and Jim Vallance, 'Dude (Looks Like a Lady)', written by Steven Tyler, Joe Perry and Desmond Child, and 'St. John' written by Steven Tyler. Side two started with 'Hangman Jury' written by Steven Tyler, Joe Perry and Jim Vallance, then 'Girl Keeps Coming Apart' written by Steven Tyler and Joe Perry, 'Angel' written by Steven Tyler and Desmond Child, 'Permanent Vacation' written by Steven Tyler and Brad Whitford, 'I'm Down' (The Beatles cover) written by John Lennon and Paul McCartney and 'The Movie' written by Steven Tyler, Joe Perry, Brad Whitford, Tom Hamilton and Joey Kramer. Four tracks were scheduled as singles: 'Hangman Jury' released first on August 18, 1987, followed by 'Dude (Looks Like a Lady)' in September 1987, 'Angel' in January 1988 and 'Rag Doll' in May 1988.

'Hangman Jury' was released as the promotional single in August with the album to follow around a week later. The track was again written by Steven Tyler and Joe Perry, and for the first time an outside collaborator, Jim Vallance, who was and remained the main writing partner for Bryan Adams. The song reverts back to blues and is an actual re-working of an old blues song that was

56

used by numerous artists over the years. Two blues artists in particular used the track in the past: Lead Belly and Taj Mahal. Steven Tyler received permission from Taj Mahal to use the refrain, but he did not receive permission from Lead Belly. However, after Lead Belly recorded it, he claimed ownership of the song. Subsequently, Lead Belly's estate sued Aerosmith about a year after 'Hangman Jury' was released. The track itself was released to rock radio in August 1987 and climbed to number 14 on the Mainstream Rock Tracks Chart. It stayed there for over 12 weeks.

The album was now released and instantly became a huge hit and a pinnacle turn for the band. On the back of 'Walk This Way', which brought them a newfound audience, *Permanent Vacation* became an album that transformed Aerosmith into the mainstream. It enjoyed constant promotion from heavy music video airplay on MTV. Although *Done with Mirrors* was the album intended as the big comeback for the band it was *Permanent Vacation* which proved to be the one that gave them the popular album they had wanted since they re-formed as the original line up. 'Rag Doll', 'Dude (Looks Like a Lady)', and 'Angel' became major hits, with all three charting within the top 20, and the accompanying music videos enjoying constant exposure through the now massive MTV helped *Permanent Vacation* become the band's greatest success in a decade. With the band also cleaning themselves up they were now a formidable force. Steven Tyler later conceded that the videos recorded around this time were the first ones he did sober. The album would go on to sell over five million copies. In addition, in the UK, it was the first Aerosmith album to attain both silver (60,000 units sold) and gold (100,000 units sold) certification by the British Phonographic Industry, achieving these in July 1989 and March 1990 respectively. Now the band had a truly global reach and were on the way to becoming one of the biggest rock bands on the planet. By 1995 the album had gone five times platinum.

With the album high in the charts and the singles giving the band further promotion and exposure all over TV and radio it was time to capitalise on this newfound success and tour once more. The Permanent Vacation Tour started in October 1987 and ran all the way through until September 1988. The band consistently played six tracks from *Permanent Vacation*: the major singles 'Dude (Looks Like a Lady)', 'Angel', and 'Rag Doll', as well as the rock radio hit 'Hangman Jury', the rocking title track, and the Beatles cover 'I'm Down'. The band also played numerous songs from their classic 1973–1982 era. A typical set list on the tour would be 'Toys in the Attic', 'Same Old Song and Dance', 'Big Ten Inch Record', 'Dude (Looks Like a Lady)', 'Lightning Strikes', 'Rag Doll', 'Hangman Jury', 'Permanent Vacation', 'Angel', 'Back in the Saddle', 'Last Child', 'Draw the Line', 'Rats in the Cellar', 'One Way Street', 'Dream On', 'Train Kept A-Rollin', 'Sweet Emotion', 'I'm Down' and 'Walk This Way'.

It was a new tour for the band in respect to their attitude to performing. It was the first since completing drug rehabilitation so they were wanting to stay clear of any drugs while the tour progressed. Guns N' Roses, who were also notorious for drug abuse at the time, were the support for part of the tour. Aerosmith asked Guns to not do drugs in their presence, so they wouldn't relapse. Guns were very much moulded in the style of Aerosmith and were heavily influenced by them, and they were also signed to same label, Geffen Records. The music video for 'Paradise City' by Guns N' Roses actually included footage from a show in which they opened for Aerosmith at Giants Stadium on August 16, 1988. Duff McKagen from the band can be seen wearing an Aerosmith T-shirt in the video. Other support acts on the tour were Extreme, Dokken and White Lion. During the tour there was also a music video created, *Permanent Vacation 3x5*. This was a VHS video featuring the music videos for 'Dude (Looks Like a Lady)', 'Angel' and 'Rag Doll'. Released in August 1988, towards the end of the tour, it also included behind-the-scenes footage from the making of those videos.

The first leg of the tour started in New York on October 16th. The band played for three nights in the city before moving to Canada for two shows in Toronto and Montreal. They then continued through North America right up until the end of the year, playing a show nearly every night. The last show of the year was in Massachusetts on December 31st; the band played three shows here on December 28th, 30th and 31st, each time to around 35,000 fans. They resumed in North America on January 16th in Seattle before again playing a gruelling run of concerts right up until the end of February, on the 28th in New Orleans. Again, they rarely missed a night as they toured. Resuming in March for the third leg they started in Virginia on the 21st taking them all the way until the end of May, ending the final leg of this section on the 22nd May at the Tingley Coliseum in Albuquerque, New Mexico. In June the tour reached Asia for six shows: they played Nagoya, Osaka, Yokohama and Tokyo where they played three shows at Nippon Budakan. They returned again to North America for the last run starting in Hawaii in June and taking them all the way through to September, where they ended the tour in California with two nights at The Pacific Amphitheatre. The tour had been an incredible success and put Aerosmith on the world map. They had played an astonishing 147 shows over five legs from October 1987 through to September 1988.

The band were now in a new phase of their career. They were back together and enjoying widespread notoriety as a class live band; this had always been there but now they had a major hit album and massive singles from it dominating the charts. They were also on heavy rotation on MTV for their music videos. Aerosmith were now in a place that gave a perfect crossover for them. 'Walk this Way', released a year earlier in 1986, gave them a huge new audience: it opened them up and crossed the genres of music. This gave them an audience who had never even heard of the band and increased their exposure. The new album in 1987 had added to that exposure, and rock fans all over the world suddenly took notice. In the UK the band were just being discovered by the mainstream as the back catalogue had previously been in the most part unavailable. Rock fans and new fans now started to do what everyone does when discovering a new artist or band for the first time: they go backwards. They trawl through the back catalogue and look for other albums that have previously been released. For new Aerosmith fans this was an incredible treat, probably more than with any other rock band; if you discovered Aerosmith in 1987 and casually looked back at their past work, it would be a revelation, a raw treasure chest of a musical rock discovery. Their back catalogue of albums was a wonderful find and gave them that edge above the competition. They had been there, they had done it all, and they had come out the other side. New bands looked at them with respect: the bad boys from Boston were exactly that, they were the real deal, and now with this tour and the newfound notoriety they were well and truly on their way to becoming one of the biggest rock bands on the planet. They were ready to rock, and Pumped Up.

Pumped Up

With only a few months' break after the end of The Permanent Vacation Tour Aerosmith returned once again to the studio, now riding high on the success they had achieved over the past two years. They joined Rik Tinory Productions in December 1988, based in Massachusetts, to work on new tracks. The studio was pretty isolated and the band wanted no outside interference or distractions as they rehearsed and composed new songs. Rik Tinory himself was self-taught as a musician and came from a very poor family. He worked his way out of poverty and performed throughout the US and around the world. In 1959 he became the first American singer/ performer to be invited to Havana, Cuba after the Cuban revolution by world heavyweight Joe Louis. In 1960 he opened his state-of-the-art 24 track recording studio, calling it Rik Tinory Productions. He recorded many world's greats including Bob Hope and George Burns. It was Aerosmith that Rik Tinory remembers with fondness and he recalled the sessions as incredible fun. They spent the longest stay in the band's history at Rik Tinory Productions, and they worked as many as 12 -15 hours a day for two long years working on tracks that would eventually become *Pump*. They also dedicated the same amount of time afterwards to songs that would later become *Get A Grip*.

In January 1989 the band again relocated to Vancouver at Fairbairn's Little Mountain Sound. They again opted for producer Bruce Fairbairn to work with and after the sessions came away with over 19 songs completed which they then considered for hits, B-sides or album tracks. Bruce Fairbairn wanted as many hooks as possible on the tracks to increase the appeal. As a result of the filtering from the songs recorded, some of them were never

61

released. These included 'Girl's Got Somethin', 'Is Anybody Out There', 'Guilty Kilt', 'Rubber Bandit', 'Sniffin' and 'Sedona Sunrise'. Many songs also had alternate titles, for example, 'Voodoo Medicine Man' was originally titled 'Buried Alive' and 'News For Ya Baby'. The majority of these songs can be seen in photos of the studio's whiteboard and in footage from *The Making of Pump*, which was a video documentary on the recording, released later in 1990.

Permanent Vacation had been a very glossy record and the brief this time from the band was for a rawer sounding album. Bruce Fairbairn had had a huge amount of success with Bon Jovi, but Steven Tyler admitted he had never listened to them so couldn't comment on any particular sound. They just wanted an element of gloss taken off and to 'strip off a little fat' that they felt was on the last record. They weren't following anyone else and were not following any traditional rules; they were just looking for something to fit. This led to musical instrumental interludes between the songs, something the band had not done before; they were added with the collaboration of musician Randy Raine-Reusch. Steven Tyler and Joe Perry had invited him to the studio after they had visited his house looking for unusual instruments to use on the album.

Lyrically it's awash with sexual themes. Steven Tyler said at the time that this was to make up for the lost time in the 1970s when he used drugs instead of having sex. The album name was discussed and eventually *Pump* was agreed on. It referenced the band being 'pumped up' now that they were clean and off drugs. The sexual nature and drug references within the lyrics was one reason why the lyrics were not added to the album booklet, which was the standard practice at the time. The label, Geffen, were concerned that there would be protests on the content from groups such as the Parents Music Resource Centre. Steven Tyler later said he regretted not adding the lyrics to the booklet. They were added however to the following tour programme. The album cover was a black and white photo of a smaller International truck known as a K Series; this was on top of a larger International truck known as a KB Series. The letters F.I.N.E. (an acronym for 'Fucked Up, Insecure, Neurotic, and Emotional') were shown as markings on the side of both hoods. The acronym was also shown in the album notes. As before, upon release the album was heavily promoted by MTV. The final selection from the recording sessions was agreed and listed as: 'Lust' written by Steven Tyler, Joe Perry and Jim Vallance, 'F.I.N.E.' written by Steven Tyler, Joe Perry and Desmond Child, 'Going Down/Love in an Elevator' written by Steven Tyler and Joe Perry, 'Monkey On My Back' written by Steven Tyler and Joe Perry, 'Water Song/Janie's Got a Gun' written by Steven Tyler and Tom Hamilton. Side two had 'Dulcimer Stomp/The Other Side' written by Steven Tyler, Jim Vallance, Brian Holland, Lamont Dozier and Eddie Holland, 'My Girl' written by Steven Tyler, Joe Perry, 'Don't Get Mad, Get Even' written by Steven Tyler and Joe Perry, 'Hoodoo/Voodoo Medicine Man' written by Steven Tyler and Brad Whitford and the final track 'What It Takes' written by Steven Tyler, Joe Perry, and Desmond Child. There was an alternative version which was made available: this also contained the track 'What It Takes' and includes an instrumental hidden track composed and performed by Randy Raine-Reusch. The Japanese version also came with 'Ain't Enough' written by Steven Tyler and Joe Perry.

As well as the additional writers that the band had worked with previously there were two other names added: Lamont Dozier and Eddie Holland. The band were subjected to a couple of lawsuits on the release of *Pump*. Firstly, a small rock band named Pump sued Aerosmith's management company for service mark infringement; however, Aerosmith won the case. Regarding the track 'The Other Side' the songwriting team of Holland–Dozier–Holland threatened to sue the band over the main melody in the song. They claimed it sounded similar to the melody in their song 'Standing in the Shadows of Love'. As part of the settlement, Aerosmith agreed to add 'Holland–Dozier–Holland' to the songwriting credits for 'The Other Side', which is why they appear in the credits on the album.

A month before the release of the album Aerosmith released the first single 'Love in an Elevator'. The track gave them another huge hit. It peaked at number five on the Billboard Hot 100 and reached number one on the Hot Mainstream Rock Tracks Chart. It also charted high in the UK and around the world, giving the band another great boost ahead of the album. Aerosmith were well and truly now established within the mainstream chart system and visual airplay around the world. The back catalogue was now also gaining momentum as new fans searched out and bought the past albums and singles, which now became sought after and highly collectable. On the 45 for 'Love in an Elevator' the song came with 'Young Lust', whereas the CD single had 'Ain't Enough' and 'Young Lust' as additional tracks. The song's lyrics were inspired by a real-life situation involving Steven Tyler in an elevator when the doors 'unexpectedly' opened. The song received a Grammy award nomination in 1990 for Best Rock Performance by a Duo or Group with Vocal. The album's other singles, 'Janie's Got a Gun', 'What It Takes' and 'The Other Side' were also huge worldwide hits. Two other singles scheduled for release were promos only: 'F.I.N.E.' and 'Monkey On My Back'.

Pump was officially released in September 1989 and stands as the band's tenth studio album. Later in 2001 it was remastered and reissued. *Pump* for the first time used a lot of keyboards and a horn section, particularly on the singles 'Love in an Elevator' and 'The Other Side'. This gave it a chart appeal that crossed over more into mainstream radio. Of course, as it's Aerosmith you don't need to look far beyond the singles to find straightforward rock songs, 'F.I.N.E.' and 'Young Lust' being good examples. The album was an incredible success and shot up the charts all over the world: it would go on to be certified for sales of over seven million copies in the US and would remain as one of the band's biggest selling albums. It also gave a huge resurgence to the past albums, pushing them forward as appetite increased for the band's legendary back catalogue of material. The band also enjoyed their first Grammy Award for 'Janie's Got a Gun' while 'Love in an Elevator' became the first Aerosmith song to hit number one on the Mainstream Rock Tracks Chart. The album gave Aerosmith three Top 10 singles on the Billboard Hot 100 and three number one singles on the Mainstream Rock Tracks Chart. It went on to be one of the bestselling albums of 1990. In the UK, it was the second Aerosmith album to be certified silver, for 60,000 units sold, by the British Phonographic Industry, achieving this in September 1989. The new set up of additional writers and the new production team of

Bruce Fairbairn with engineers Mike Fraser and Ken Lomas at The Little Mountain Sound Studios was proving a winning formula for the band. A video documentary on the recording, *The Making of Pump*, was released later in 1990.

The next tour for the band was on a truly global scale. They were now one of the biggest, if not *the* biggest, rock bands on the planet. The Pump Tour lasted for a whole year from mid-October 1989 to mid-October 1990. Significantly the tour gave the band its first return to Europe since 1977, as well as the first-ever performances in Australia. In addition, this tour saw the band tour North America on numerous legs, as well as perform a series of dates in Japan. The opening acts were also huge acts in their own right, but such was Aerosmith's standing at the time any rock band's kudos was instantly lifted when associated with them. Opening support acts included Skid Row, Joan Jett, The Cult, Poison, Warrant, Metallica, The Black Crowes and The Quireboys. Some of these acts were regular openers, while some opened for Aerosmith only at specific festivals or stadium shows. Such was the band's success at this time that they had their own plane for the tour. They used a Citation II private plane, which they renamed 'Aeroforce One'. The plane was formerly used by Philippine dictator Ferdinand Marcos.

The tour was split into several legs. The set list loosely followed the following format: 'Heart's Done Time', 'Young Lust', 'F.I.N.E.', 'Monkey On My Back', 'Don't Get Mad, Get Even', 'Janie's Got a Gun', 'Permanent Vacation', 'Mama Kin', 'What It Takes', 'Voodoo Medicine Man', 'Red House' (The Jimi Hendrix Experience cover), 'Draw the Line', 'Rag Doll', 'Sweet Emotion', 'Dude (Looks Like a Lady)', 'Dream On', 'Love in an Elevator'. The band typically played two encores, 'Train Kept A-Rollin' and of course 'Walk This Way'. The tour kicked off in Europe with a concert in Cologne, Germany on October 18th 1989 before moving onto Italy, France, Belgium, the Netherlands and Germany for eight more concerts, Denmark, Sweden, England, Scotland, Northern Ireland, and a return to England at Wembley on November 26th. The next leg of the tour covered North America and Canada, taking them from December 15th 1989 through to July 28th 1990 at Maryland. On February 21, 1990, the band appeared in a 'Wayne's World' sketch on *Saturday Night Live*, debating the fall of communism and the Soviet Union, and performed their recent hits 'Janie's Got a Gun' and 'Monkey On My Back'. The appearance on 'Wayne's World' was later ranked by *E!* as the number-one moment in the history of the program. The band would return later to 'Wayne's World' for the second instalment in the movie franchise. The next leg of the tour started back in Europe where demand was incredible for the band; they started in Dublin on August 15th 1990 before playing Castle Donington and London. They then toured around Europe once more until September 3rd with a final concert in Paris. The band played in Vegas on September 8th before heading for Japan for the next phase. They played Osaka, Nagasaki, Yokohama and Tokyo, finishing on September 22nd. The final leg of the tour took them for the first time to Australia, where they played six concerts starting on September 29th in Adelaide. The tour concluded in Perth on October 15th 1990. In all the band played a total of 164 shows over the course of the tour. Aerosmith were now on an all-time high, widely considered to be the biggest and best rock band in the world by those who saw them perform live.

During the tour more highlights took place for the band. Steven Tyler met Mick Jagger and the band met Robert Plant and Jimmy Page, who saw the band perform on separate occasions in England. At one show, Page jammed with the band on 'Train Kept A-Rollin', and at another show he played an extended set with the band at the Marquee Club in London. They also during the tour recorded special performances on the *Howard Stern Show* and *Saturday Night Live*. Towards the end of the tour the band also recorded an *MTV Unplugged* session which was a huge deal at the time. Unlike most of the artists who had appeared for an *MTV Unplugged* session Aerosmith didn't release an album of the performance. They only performed one song from *Permanent Vacation* and *Pump* opting instead to perform lesser known songs from their back catalogue, songs such as 'Seasons of Wither' and 'One Way Street'. They also chose some covers, returning to their blues roots from the past fifteen years.

At the end of 1990 Aerosmith were in a place where only a few rock bands can get to. They were quite rightly inducted into the Hollywood Rock Walk for their contributions and they sat now as world stars. They were respected, adored and filling out huge arenas all over the planet. Their last two albums had catapulted them into the mainstream and, with the quality of their back catalogue, they garnered respect from all other bands at the time, particularly new bands trying to break through. The band now took a break, but not before capitalising on their incredible back catalogue of material. They worked through this planning a set that would showcase it in all its glory. The set would be an incredible statement from the band and would further capitalise on their newfound success. If there was ever a musical statement to showcase an incredible back catalogue, this was it: Gotta Love it.

On the Edge

In 1991 the band worked through putting together a compilation album of their past songs spanning the period from the 1970s to the early 1980s. The box set was released in November 1991 and was named *Pandora's Box*. It was issued by Columbia Records to capitalise on the band's newfound success with Geffen. The set covers an incredible period from the band, spanning three discs that cover Aerosmith's output from the 1970s and early 1980s. There were also many alternate versions, previously unreleased songs, live renditions and remixes. There was an original issue that had a long cardboard box, containing the three CDs with each having its own jewel-case. It also had a booklet that detailed the tracks with various comments from the band and extra information. There were later reissues of the set that had a different case and reproduced the booklet in CD size. To promote the box set the band rereleased 'Sweet Emotion' and a music video was created to promote the single. As expected, the box set became extremely collectable.

MTV in 1991 was celebrating its tenth anniversary. They ran a special and Aerosmith performed their 1973 single 'Dream On' alongside Michael Kamen's orchestra. The performance was used as the official music video for the song.

In January 1992 the band went back into A&M Studios in Santa Monica, California to start work on what would be their next album. With these sessions completed they then returned to Little Mountain Sound Studios from September to complete the tracks. The album was to be named *Get a Grip*, and would be their eleventh studio album. It would go on to be the biggest selling album yet for the band. Aerosmith chose twelve tracks initially for the album and wanted to release it at the back end of 1992. John

Kalodner was a Geffen A&R man at the time and thought that the album needed more radio friendly tunes, so with this in mind the band returned to the studio to write more tracks and as before worked with outside collaborators such as Desmond Child. Because of the amount of songs the band ended up recording, many from these sessions were used as B-sides going forward, or indeed were never actually released at all: 'Don't Stop' and 'Head First' were released as B-sides whereas 'Can't Stop Messin'' would go on to appear on several special editions as an additional track. Other songs were listed on the official Aerosmith website in the late 1990s. 'Black Cherry', 'Devil's Got A New Disguise', 'Dime Store Lover', 'Legendary Child', 'Lizard Love', 'Meltdown', 'Rocket 88', 'Wham Bam' and 'Yo Momma' were all listed on the lyrics page of the website. Many of the recorded songs from these sessions have since been released on various albums and soundtracks.

The final track list for *Get a Grip* was decided: 'Intro' written by Steven Tyler, Joe Perry and Jim Vallance, 'Eat the Rich' written by Steven Tyler, Joe Perry and Jim Vallance, 'Get a Grip' written by Steven Tyler, Joe Perry and Jim Vallance, 'Fever' written by Steven Tyler and Joe Perry, 'Livin' on the Edge' written by Steven Tyler, Joe Perry and Mark Hudson, 'Flesh' written by Steven Tyler, Joe Perry and Desmond Child, 'Walk On Down' written by Joe Perry, 'Shut Up and Dance' written by Steven Tyler, Joe Perry, Jack Blades and Tommy Shaw, 'Cryin'' written by Steven Tyler, Joe Perry and Taylor Rhodes, 'Gotta Love It' written by Steven Tyler, Joe Perry and Mark Hudson, 'Crazy' written by Steven Tyler, Joe Perry and Desmond Child, 'Line Up' (featuring Lenny Kravitz) written by Steven Tyler, Joe Perry, and Lenny Kravitz, 'Amazing' written by Steven Tyler and Richard Supa and 'Boogie Man (Instrumental)' written by Steven Tyler, Joe Perry and Jim Vallance. The album was divided into four sides with the UK version having 'Can't Stop Messin'' as track 13. A huge seven singles in total were scheduled for release, showing the band's and label's continued hunger for chart hits: 'Livin' on the Edge' was the first release on March 23, 1993, then 'Eat the Rich' on April 17, 1993, 'Cryin'' on October 5, 1993, 'Amazing' and 'Line Up' both released in November 1993, 'Shut Up and Dance' in January 1994 (in the UK only) and finally 'Crazy', released in May 1994.

The first single, released in March a month ahead of the album, gave another huge hit for the band. 'Livin' on the Edge' was another massive single for Aerosmith and landed high in many charts. Now the standard Billboard chart was becoming stretched and various breakaway charts were emerging. It reached number 18 on the Billboard Hot 100 chart, number three on the Cash Box Top 100, and number one on the Billboard Album Rock Tracks Chart, where it remained for nine weeks. This made it Aerosmith's most successful single on that chart. In the UK, the song peaked at number 19 on the British pop chart in April 1993, giving the band even more exposure. The music video also helped the track and the promotion of the new record. It's a violent one and features grand theft auto, joyriding and all sorts of disruption among school-aged youth. It also shows cross-dressing teachers, and a naked Steven Tyler holding a zipper by his crotch with half his body painted black (to give the effect he pulled down a zipper, unzipping his body). At one point Joe Perry plays a lead guitar solo in front of an oncoming train; this scene was filmed on Lake Britton Bridge in Shasta County, California, the same bridge where the famous train scene in *Stand By Me* was filmed. The video was directed by Marty Callner. It also featured *Terminator 2* actor Edward Furlong and really gives an insight into the band's appeal at the time. 'Livin' on the Edge' became a well embedded staple for any following tours and became a fan favourite when played live. The song won Aerosmith another Grammy Award for Best Rock Performance by A Duo or Group with Vocal for the year 1993. The video went on to win a Viewers' Choice award at the 1993 MTV Video Music Awards and was also voted Best Video by *Metal Edge* readers in the magazine's 1993 Readers' Choice Awards.

The band on the back of 'Livin' on the Edge' were now poised to release *Get a Grip*. They were now in a truly iconic place. They had the perfect balance for any rock band. They had, in the past, released raw albums of pure rock, albums that were back to basics and homed in on all the traditions of blues and rock music, blending them in a unique way, giving Aerosmith a signature sound. Whether they liked it or not the fusion of drink and drugs had incentivised and sculpted the sound; it also gave them a reputation on the road and in their live performances that was legendary. They had literally seen it and done it all. In addition, this had threatened the very fabric of the band and for a few years they had gone their separate ways on different projects. This added to the appeal when the band finally regrouped and ultimately got clean. They now, with additional songwriters, changed the writing slightly, adding embellishments and hooks going after the mainstream charts, and it worked. They were now, in music terms, household names, and they were being discovered; with the immense back catalogue, they were becoming explored and for music fans this was a revelation. They had a story to tell and it was musically, commercially and culturally fascinating. There was not a band around that had such an incredible back story of rise and fall, and one that had such a variety and incredible contribution to the discovery of rock music.

Get a Grip was released on April 20, 1993 by Geffen Records. It would be band's last studio album on the label before they returned to Columbia Records. The album also featured guests including Don Henley, who sang backup on 'Amazing', and Lenny Kravitz, who offered backup vocals and collaboration to 'Line Up'. Sticking to the now trusted and winning formulas, as with both *Permanent Vacation* and *Pump, Get a Grip* featured a whole host of song collaborators from outside the band. It was a substantial list but the main players who contributed were Desmond Child, Jim Vallance, Mark Hudson, Richie Supa, Taylor Rhodes, Jack Blades, and Tommy Shaw.

Remarkably, *Get a Grip* superseded both *Permanent Vacation* and *Pump*. It became Aerosmith's best-selling studio album worldwide, eventually achieving an incredible statistic of over 20 million copies sold. It was just as successful as *Pump* in the US, reaching over seven million copies, and continued to rise. *Toys in the Attic* also had a huge resurgence and moved forward to top eight million in the following years. This also made it their third consecutive album with US sales of at least five million. Two songs from the album won Grammy Awards for Best Rock Performance by a Duo or Group with Vocal; these were awarded for 'Livin' on the Edge' and 'Crazy' . The album was also voted

81

Album of the Year by *Metal Edge* readers in the magazine's 1993 Readers' Choice Awards, while 'Livin' on the Edge' was voted the Best Video.

Musically, around this time in 1993 there were significant changes in mainstream popular music. Things were moving fast and to stay relevant you had to work hard within popular culture. Aerosmith weren't young and had to commercially keep themselves viable in the fast consumable markets of music and its cultural associated areas. This naturally gave a double edged conflict within what the band were doing. There were many critics who were underwhelmed with the direction the band were taking, especially on the release and commercialisation of power-ballads in promoting their albums. Although all three tracks, 'Cryin', 'Amazing', and 'Crazy', were all massive successes on radio and MTV, many people said that they had sold out for purely commercial gains. The music videos featured Alicia Silverstone and her provocative performances earned her the title of 'the Aerosmith chick' for much of the 1990s. Also, Steven Tyler's own daughter Liv Tyler was featured in the 'Crazy' video.

The band next planned a tour to commence in June 1993, but to capitalise further and gain increased recognition in the fast-moving changing word of popular music, they sought to exploit youth culture to the max. The band recorded scenes in the second instalment of the 'Wayne's World' franchise, *Wayne's World 2*. The film, adapted by Mike Myers from *Saturday Night Live* sketches, features the band as themselves. The subsequent soundtrack to the movie also featured 'Shut Up and Dance' from *Get a Grip*; it was the live version that was actually included on the soundtrack to the movie. It also included 'Dude (Looks Like a Lady)'. The movie was released in November 1993.

The band also increased their exposure within youth culture by capitalising on the increasing gaming business. The *Revolution X* game was developed and published by Midway in 1994 and featured Aerosmith. The gameplay was very similar to another game recently released by Midway, which was the *Terminator 2: Judgment Day* game. In the game, players battle the oppressive New Order Nation regime and their leader Helga, who have abducted Aerosmith. Players use a mounted gun to control onscreen crosshairs and shoot enemies using compact discs. The members of Aerosmith are hidden throughout the game's international locations and must be found in order to receive the game's true ending. The game became a critical and commercial success. In addition, the band also contributed to the video game *Quest for Fame* which was an early simulation game where the player becomes a rock guitarist, working his way up from lonesome bedroom rehearsals to becoming a garage band member, playing clubs and ultimately becoming a rock legend. The game was based on tunes by Aerosmith. A very limited game engine was included on a CD-ROM track on Aerosmith's *Nine Lives* and also included drum tracks for the very first time in a Virtual Music title. The above games were launched and became extremely successful as simultaneously Aerosmith embarked on the biggest and most gruelling tour of their career.

The Get a Grip Tour began on June 2nd 1993 in Topeka, Kansas. It went right through until December 19th 1994. It covered an incredible 13 legs and 240 live shows. The set list as expected covered the band's history and was littered with concert favourites from the growing list of concert staples; the set list loosely ran as follows: 'Intro', 'Eat the Rich', 'Toys in the Attic', 'Fever', 'What it Takes', 'Amazing', 'Rag Doll', 'Cryin'', 'Mama Kin', 'Shut Up and Dance', 'Walk on Down', 'Janie's Got a Gun', 'Love in an Elevator', 'Dude (Looks Like a Lady)', 'Sweet Emotion', 'Dream On', 'Livin' on the Edge' and 'Walk This Way'. The final concert finished the run at the band's Mama Kin's Music Hall in Boston, the club they had purchased and renamed. Along the way the band played some special shows between their main dates which included a number of television performances on programmes such as *Saturday Night Live*, the *Late Show with David Letterman*, *MTV's Most Wanted*, the MTV Video Music Awards, the Grammy Awards, and the MTV Europe Music Awards. The band also played a few club shows, in Los Angeles, London, and a surprise show at a local club in Sioux Falls, South Dakota after a concert there. Notably also was the band's performance at the Woodstock '94 festival which took place in August 1994. The band closed the show on Saturday night taking the stage later than planned, at around 1:15am. They played in front of an estimated crowd of

350,000 people. The band was originally supposed to start at midnight, but due to a heavy downpour the start time was delayed. Both Steven Tyler and Joey Kramer had attended the original Woodstock Festival in 1969.

The tour became one of longest in the band's history alongside the Nine Lives Tour, which lasted for three years. It held the record for the most shows ever performed by Aerosmith on a single tour. The sections of the tour covered North America, Europe, Japan, and Central and South America. The tour marked the band's first performances in Central and South America, as well as in a number of European nations, including Romania, Hungary, Poland, Russia, Turkey, Israel, Spain, Finland, Norway, the Czech Republic, and Austria. There was a whole host of bands who joined the tour as opening acts; these included Megadeth, Mighty Bosstones, Cry of Love, Jackyl, 4 Non Blondes, Soul Asylum, Therapy?, Collective Soul, Extreme, Brother Cane, Mr. Big and Robert Plant in Argentina. There was some controversy surrounding Megadeth, who had opened the first shows in June, but Aerosmith fired as them after they overheard Megadeath's lead vocalist Dave Mustaine disrespecting them in a radio interview.

By the end of this mammoth tour, *Get a Grip* had gone on to sell over twelve million records worldwide; it reached over seven million copies sold in the United States alone. The album had charted four Top 40 hits, and won the band two Grammy Awards, four MTV Video Music Awards, two People's Choice Awards, two American Music Awards, and a Billboard Award. To increase things even further, if it was ever needed at this time, Aerosmith released a compilation album through Geffen, which was released towards the end of the tour, in November 1994. The album, *Big Ones*, also included two new songs they had written, 'Blind Man' and 'Walk on Water', and as a result these two songs were also included in the set list during the final days of the tour. Those two tracks were recorded at a hotel on the island of Capri in July 1994, after the band's summer leg of dates in Europe. *Big Ones* featured 12 hits from the band's three consecutive multi-platinum albums, *Permanent Vacation* (1987), *Pump* (1989), and the new release *Get a Grip* in 1993. It also included the hit 'Deuces are Wild' which was featured on *The Beavis and Butt-Head Experience* released in November 1993.

The Beavis and Butt-Head Experience was a compilation album released in 1993 also by Geffen Records. The name is a reference to Jimi Hendrix's original band, The Jimi Hendrix Experience, and it became one of the bestselling comedy albums: it went on to sell over 1.5 million records and became certified double platinum by the RIAA in the United States. In 2016, the album was reissued on vinyl, in picture disc form.

The two new songs added to *Big Ones*, 'Blind Man' and 'Walk on Water', were recorded during a break in the Get a Grip Tour. These songs were also included on the band's 2001 compilation album, *Young Lust: The Aerosmith Anthology*. *Big Ones* went on to become one of the biggest and best-selling compilation albums. It reached number six on the Billboard charts, going on to sell over four million albums. To conclude the huge tour the band closed it with a fitting performance at their recently opened Mama Kin's Music Hall in Boston on December 19, 1994. The performance was changed to the standard set and showcased more of the band's 1970s classics. It was broadcast on radio across North America.

Get a Grip and the tour that followed cemented Aerosmith as the biggest rock band in the world. The constant hits and the ability to release compilation albums of their past songs gave them an incredible ability to showcase their formidable career in rock music and live shows. Every time they went into the studio during this period, they produced an album that was massive, and massive all over the world. Other bands and critics thought at every point in their career that they were finished, that the tour they were on was some sort of farewell tour and the album they were working on would be their last. Aerosmith however were going nowhere; they were at this point in time unstoppable. They had survived every feasible obstacle that could be thrown at them and come back stronger each time. Where other bands would have ended, Aerosmith had proved they had more than Nine Lives.

Don't Miss a Thing

After a short break Aerosmith reconvened to produce what would be their twelfth studio album, *Nine Lives*. They were between the two labels at this moment: Geffen and Columbia. The band had signed a reported $30 million contract covering four albums with Columbia Records/Sony Music in 1991 but at this point they had only recorded three of their six contractual albums with Geffen Records, which were *Done with Mirrors*, *Permanent Vacation* and *Pump*. Between 1991 and 1996 they had released two more albums with Geffen, which were *Get a Grip* and the compilation album *Big Ones*. This meant that they now had five albums with Geffen under their belt (along with a planned live compilation) and now they could now begin recording for their new contract with Columbia.

The initial recordings started at Criteria Studios in Miami, Florida. They worked with producer Glen Ballard. It was here that Steven Tyler and Glen Ballard co-wrote the lyrics for 'Falling in Love (Is Hard on the Knees)', 'Taste of India' and 'Pink'. As usual there were additional collaborators, including Desmond Child and Taylor Rhodes, who joined Steven Tyler and Joe Perry to write songs. Desmond Childs himself had now contributed to many Aerosmith hits including 'Angel,' 'Crazy' and 'Dude (Looks like a Lady)' amongst others.

The band had an issue before the main rehearsals. Drummer Joey Kramer was suffering from depression; he was grieving the loss of his father a few years before and was now unavailable. Again, with this news it was rumoured that the band would be coming to an end. Steve Ferrone was brought in to play drums while Joey Kramer went through recovery. When he did return the band rerecorded from scratch the entire album so as to keep the Aerosmith sound, which some thought was lost originally while Joey Kramer was away. When the band showcased the nine tracks they had recorded, Columbia were dissatisfied, and the album was delayed from its scheduled release for the summer of 1996. Adding to the delay, the band asked their long serving manager Tim Collins to step down. He had been with Aerosmith for nearly twelve years up until this point. Joe Perry himself had stated that he felt Tim Collins was pitting the band members against each other and that he felt betrayed by him. With Tim Collins gone the band hired producer Kevin Shirley, who had previously worked with Journey, and set up at Avatar Studios in New York City. The band now worked towards getting the sound they wanted with overtones and instruments, paying particular attention to the guitar sounds, and in the end they were happy with the result, which they felt was somewhere between *Toys in the Attic* and *Rocks*.

Following on the new sessions began in September 1996, continuing through until November. The band ended up with 24 songs. A Columbia A&R executive was brought back to check progress and the 24 was trimmed down to 13. The band wanted initially to call the album *Vindaloo* after adding and being influenced by Indian music throughout some of the songs, including a sarangi intro by Ramesh Mishra on the song 'Taste of India'; however, when they completing the track 'Nine Lives', the band felt that would make the perfect title, kind of representing the album's difficult beginnings up to this point.

The thirteen tracks were whittled down to 'Nine Lives' written by Steven Tyler, Joe Perry and Marti Frederiksen, 'Falling in Love (Is Hard on the Knees)' written by Steven Tyler, Joe Perry, and Glen Ballard, 'Hole in My Soul' written by Steven Tyler, Joe Perry and Desmond Child, ' A Taste of India' written by Steven Tyler, Joe Perry and Glen Ballard, 'Full Circle' written by Steven Tyler and Taylor Rhodes, 'Something's Gotta Give' written by Steven Tyler, Joe Perry and Marti Frederiksen, 'Ain't That a Bitch' written by Steven Tyler, Joe Perry and Desmond Child, 'The Farm' written by Steven Tyler, Joe Perry, Mark Hudson and Steve Dudas, 'Crash' written by Steven Tyler, Joe Perry, Mark Hudson and Dominic Miller, 'Kiss Your Past Good-Bye' written by Steven

Tyler and Mark Hudson, 'Pink' written by Steve Tyler, Richard Supa and Glen Ballard, 'Attitude Adjustment' written by Steven Tyler, Joe Perry and Marti Frederiksen and 'Fallen Angels' written by Steven Tyler, Joe Perry and Richard Supa. There were also international bonus tracks which were 'Falling Off', 'Attitude Adjustment' and 'Fallen Angels'. In Japan there were two additional tracks released, 'Falling Off' and 'Fall Together', and in South America the album also had 'Falling Off', 'Attitude Adjustment', 'Fallen Angels' and 'I Don't Want to Miss a Thing'. This was also the case for the later re-release.

The first single scheduled for release was 'Falling in Love (Is Hard on the Knees)', which was scheduled for February 1997, a month before the actual album. The song was written by Steven Tyler, Joe Perry and Glen Ballard. Glen Ballard himself was signed initially to produce *Nine Lives* but he was subsequently dropped from the role halfway through production, when he was replaced by Kevin Shirley. Glen Ballard was still credited for his contributions however. He co-wrote 'Pink' with Steven Tyler and Joe Perry and also 'Taste of India' alongside Steven Tyler and Richard Supa, which is why he is still credited on the album itself. 'Falling in Love (Is Hard on the Knees)' was another hit for the band. It was a huge single in Spain topping the Spanish Singles Chart, and it also reached number two in Canada and remained there for four weeks. It topped the UK Rock Chart and the US Billboard Mainstream Rock Chart. Elsewhere, the song peaked at number seven in Finland and reached the top 30 in Poland, Sweden, Switzerland and the United Kingdom. On the US Billboard Hot 100, it reached number 35, becoming the second highest-charting song from the album on that chart, after 'Pink'. With the single giving a good piece of promotion it was now time for Aerosmith to release the album itself.

Released on March 18th 1997, *Nine Lives* reached number one on the Billboard Top 200. One of the album's singles, 'Pink', won a Grammy Award for Best Rock Performance by a Duo or Group with Vocal. The other singles scheduled for release were dotted over the coming year and into 1997. The power ballad 'Hole in My Soul' was released in August 1997. It reached the edge of the chart at 51 on the Billboard Hot 100 and on the Mainstream

Rock Tracks Chart it peaked at number four. In the UK the song reached number 29. 'Pink' was released in November with 'Full Circle' shortly after. 'Nine Lives' itself and 'Taste of India' were released as promos only. The album itself, after peaking, fell down the charts quite quickly, but the subsequent singles and the accompanying music videos interspersed across the year kept pushing it back slightly up, keeping it going further than it would have left to its own devices.

Nine Lives would be the last studio album for Aerosmith of the decade. It was a decade that saw them return from the depths of drug and substance abuse to a worldwide commercial force in rock music. It also saw them return once again to their first record label, which prompted them to return to their core blues sound. The record had many issues and the band were now relieved that it was eventually released. It had been an arduous task to get *Nine Lives* recorded and released. In the time it took to record it they had two producers, which meant two different recording processes. They fired their manager and for a period looked like they would disband completely, and they also had other internal management and band member issues. Once they had sorted out the band again and re-grouped in September 1996, they had to record more tracks as the label were not happy with the original cut. The album was then in effect re-recorded from scratch.

As before, *Nine Lives* featured co-writers from outside the band. Critics were not overly warm towards the album upon release but it topped the US album charts and reached the Top 10 in nearly a dozen other countries, making it a worldwide hit by any commercial standard. And, of course, the momentum would not stop as the band entered the following year, which would yield another massive worldwide single during their next world tour.

Starting in May 1997 the band embarked on the Nine Lives World Tour. By any standard Aerosmith were now the ultimate kings in large scale world tours, filling out huge arenas and stadiums all over the planet. The tour would take in an incredible 204 shows, although it was scheduled for 283 with 43 cancelled and 36 rearranged. The tour would last nearly two years, taking the band right through until June 1999.

The tour covered the US, Canada, Japan, the United Kingdom, Germany, Spain, Czech Republic, Belgium, France, Switzerland, Holland, Italy, Austria, Finland, Sweden, Denmark and Portugal. As expected with such a mammoth undertaking the tour featured many support acts along the way with some opening for entire legs, others for only half. Some performers appeared at selected dates and others performed just once. These included Shed Seven, Kula Shaker, 3 Colours Red, Jonny Lang, Marry Me Jane, Talk Show, Days of the New, Kenny Wayne Shepherd, Spacehog, Monster Magnet, Fuel, Fighting Gravity, Seven Mary Three, Candlebox, The Afghan Whigs, The Black Crowes, Lenny Kravitz, Bryan Adams, Stereophonics, Skunk Anansie, Ministry and Guano Apes. There were several dates along the way that had to be rescheduled or even cancelled due to Steven Tyler suffering a ligament injury when a microphone stand fell hard onto his knee. This forced the band to cancel several dates while he recovered. The tour was obviously initially planned to promote *Nine Lives*; however, during the tour itself Aerosmith landed a huge worldwide hit single and the tour was extended to capitalise on it. The band were just wrapping up and about to come off the road when 'I Don't Want to Miss a Thing' landed. It became a monster of a single for the band and sent them back to the top of the charts.

'I Don't Want to Miss a Thing' was a rock ballad in connection to the 1998 movie *Armageddon*, which Steven Tyler's daughter Liv Tyler starred in. It was written by Diane Warren. The song debuted at number one on the US Billboard Hot 100, giving Aerosmith their first number one single there. It is one of four songs performed by the band for the film, the other three being 'What Kind Of Love Are You On', 'Come Together' and 'Sweet Emotion'. It became an incredibly successful project for them. In September 1998 the song stayed at number one for four weeks and did the same in several other countries. It sold over a million copies in the UK and reached number four on the UK Singles Chart. The track gained fast momentum and became Aerosmith's biggest hit, and introduced them once again to a new generation of fans. The power of the movie collaboration also brought a cross marketing element to the promotion: the song promoting the movie and movie promoting the song. The music video also became extremely popular, having heavy rotation on all music channels, and again it promoted the movie by having movie scenes intertwined throughout the video. While filming the music video Steven Tyler was in a cast because he was recovering from his knee injury. The original version of the song was a collaboration between Chicago musician Phil Kosch of Treaty of Paris and Super Happy Fun Club, and the nephew of chart-topping writer Lou Bega. Bega introduced the two and they penned the initial track, but ultimately Phil Kosch was uncredited. The song went on to be nominated for an Academy Award for Best Original Song. The single also took something from *Nine Lives* on the track listings to promote the album, with 'Taste of India' being added. The single came with 'I Don't Want to Miss a Thing', 'I Don't Want to Miss a Thing (Rock Mix)', 'Taste of India' also as a Rock Remix and 'Animal Crackers'. On the Argentine version and a European re-released version of the album *Nine Lives* it was also included. It also appeared on the Japanese version of *Just Push Play*. Another version of the single came with 'Pink' as a live version and 'Crash'.

With the tour continuing on the back of this success it went right through into the middle of 1999. At the start of the concerts the was some Persian music as the curtain was still closed and the crowd were getting excited for the start; this music was actually 'The Feeling Begins' by Peter Gabriel. It can be found on his *Passion* album as well as on the soundtrack to *The Last Temptation of Christ*. The show had a standard format of around 24 songs played, lasting for around 1 hour and 30 minutes. This did vary however from show to show; at one show for example only 12 songs were played. The set list varied but the following songs were played at every concert: 'Cryin', 'Dream On', 'Love in an Elevator', 'Pink', 'Sweet Emotion' and 'Walk This Way'. The title track from the new record, 'Nine Lives', was the opening song at most shows.

From late October 1998 onwards, the tour was also named The Little South of Sanity Tour, to promote the release of the Geffen live album of the same name.

A Little South of Sanity was another live album from Aerosmith, released on October 20th 1998. It served as a combined album from both Geffen Records and Columbia Records. The album covered two discs and was recorded while the band were on the Nine Lives Tour and the Get a Grip Tour. The CD came with a Parental Advisory sticker, the first time the band had had one, mainly because of Steven Tyler's language and outbursts between the songs, and because he changed some song lyrics, which included a large amount of profanities. The release of the album enabled Aerosmith to complete their contract with Geffen Records. There are no listings to support where or when each performance was taken from on the various tours except for Steven Tyler calling out to the crowds between and during the sets. The recordings of 'Love in an Elevator', 'Same Old Song and Dance' and 'Sweet Emotion' each have Tyler calling out to the live crowd; the first song has him mentioning the crowd in State College, Pennsylvania, the second a crowd in West Palm Beach, Florida, and the third a crowd in Seattle, Washington. The two discs are again an outstanding example of Aerosmith as a live force. The track listing is as follows. Disc one: 'Eat the Rich', 'Love in an Elevator', 'Falling in Love (Is Hard on the Knees)', 'Same Old Song and Dance', 'Hole in My Soul', 'Monkey on My Back', 'Livin' on the Edge', 'Cryin', 'Rag Doll', 'Angel', 'Janie's Got a Gun' and 'Amazing'. Disc Two: 'Back in the Saddle', 'Last Child', 'The Other Side',' Walk on Down', 'Dream On', 'Crazy', 'Mama Kin', 'Walk This Way', 'Dude (Looks Like a Lady)', 'What It Takes' and 'Sweet Emotion'. The album did very well and landed high in the charts around the world; in the US it peaked at number twelve on the Billboard chart and in Japan it went as high as number three. In other countries it landed around the mid to early 20s on the various chart systems.

A Little South of Sanity stood as the fourth live album by Aerosmith. It was a definitive statement to bring back to the fold classic Aerosmith tracks from the past. It went on to be their most successful live album to date, with many still calling it the band's greatest. It has truly outstanding performances with a quality track list. It mixed perfectly the standard classics with the relatively new songs; the band created a simply incredible live rock album. Aerosmith as a band were always known for their exceptional stage shows and phenomenal performances. For those who had not seen the band, or were not familiar with them, *A Little South of Sanity* was a fantastic teaser into the world of a live Aerosmith show.

With the album out showcasing the live force that the band were, and the huge success of 'I Don't Want to Miss a Thing' which led to the extension of the tour, the band were again simply huge as they closed off the two years they had spent touring and performing. The last performance of the 204 shows that the band played on the tour was on July 17th 1999 in Portugal at the T99 festival. The tour was a great success even though several dates were cancelled because of Joey Kramer and Steven Tyler recovering from serious injuries that occurred on separate occasions. They were universally praised and admired for their live shows, longevity and outstanding contribution to rock music.

There were many who thought Aerosmith were once again finished during this tour but yet again they had provided a remarkable tour covering the entire globe. The albums still kept coming, becoming huge, as well as another single that provided a worldwide hit pushing the band deep into legendary status. Aerosmith, with this tour and the release of *A Little South of Sanity* and 'I Don't Want to Miss a Thing', had again silenced the critics. They were still the biggest band in the world, still moving forward, still pushing.

Push and Play

Not content with the 204-date tour that they had just completed, Aerosmith decided to tour Japan towards the end of 1999 to see in the new year. Before this, however, on September 9th 1999 Steven Tyler and Joe Perry reunited with Run–DMC, along with Kid Rock, for a collaborative live performance of 'Walk This Way' at the MTV Video Music Awards. The Roar of the Dragon Tour lasted from 1999 through to the new year in 2000. It included a New Year/Millennium show in Osaka on December 31, 1999. Part of the show was recorded and later broadcast on ABC television; this was directed by Dick Carruthers. This would form part of the special programming for Millennium celebrations across the world. The tour was only for six dates but Aerosmith made a concerted effort to make them special and unique. The show utilised many Asian themes and represented Asian culture, including dragons. These featured on the big screens as well as into and throughout the stage set up. The tour was focused on Japan as the Nine Lives Tour only reached Japan once, being mainly focused on other territories such as North America and Europe, which it visited on several legs.

The tour included six shows in total: two shows in Osaka on December 29th and 31st 1999, one show in Nagoya on January 2nd 2000, Fukuoka on January 4th 2000 and two shows in Tokyo at the Tokyo Dome on January 6th and 7th 2000. The set list for the shows was also tweaked slightly and ran through the following: 'Eat the Rich', 'Falling in Love (Is Hard on the Knees)', 'Same Old Song and Dance', 'Love in an Elevator', 'Livin' on the Edge', 'Rag Doll', 'Dream On', 'Janie's Got a Gun', 'Lord of the Thighs' performed on 29/12/99; 'One Way Street' performed on 31/12/99;

'No More No More' performed on 1/2/00, 'Lick and a Promise' performed on 4/01/00, 1/6/00, and 7/1/00, 'Full Circle' performed on 29/12/99, 'Nothing' performed on' 31/12/99, 'Remember (Walking in the Sand)' and 'Big Ten Inch Record' performed on 2/1/00, 'Last Child' on 6/1/00 and 7/1/00, 'Pink', 'Let the Music Do the Talking', 'Draw the Line' performed on 7/1/00, 'Stop Messin' Round' with 'Red House' added as an intro for all January shows, 'Mother Popcorn', 'Walk This Way', 'I Don't Want To Miss A Thing', 'Cryin', 'Dude (Looks Like A Lady)', 'Chip Away the Stone', played only on 31/12/99, 'Mama Kin', 'Train Kept A-Rollin' on 31/12/99 only and 'Auld Lang Syne', played only on 31/12/99. The encores for the shows were 'Train Kept A-Rollin', 'What It Takes' which was dropped from the set list after 29/12/99, 'Sweet Emotion' which also included parts of 'Heartbreaker' played on 29/12/99 and 31/12/99 and parts of 'S.O.S. (Too Bad)' played on 4/1/00, 6/1/00, and 7/1/00.

The band next contributed another song to a movie about to be released. They contributed 'Angel's Eye' to the new movie *Charlie's Angels* and it appeared on the soundtrack to the film. The track was written by Steven Tyler and Joe Perry with collaborators Marti Frederiksen and Taylor Rhodes. It was released as a promotional single for the movie and again received heavy rotation on rock radio. It reached number four on the Mainstream Rock Tracks Chart giving the band another hit single attributed to a major movie. The main single from the soundtrack was from Destiny's Child; 'Independent Women' went on to be a huge hit and was also featured on the album *Survivor*, their third album, as well as on the *Charlie's Angels* soundtrack itself.

From April through to December 2000 Aerosmith returned to the studio to work on new tracks for their next album. The band released 'Jaded' as the first single from their new album, *Just Push Play*, on December 21st 2000. The track was written by Steven Tyler and Marti Frederiksen. The song was another huge success for Aerosmith and reached number one on both the US Billboard Mainstream Rock Chart and the UK Rock Chart. It also reached the top ten on the Billboard Hot 100 and in Canada. On the UK Singles Chart, the song reached number 13 and became the band's eighth top-twenty single on that chart. It was also a huge hit throughout Europe and reached the high teens and top ten in several European countries. The single's artwork caused a bit of controversy at the time, as it featured a naked woman holding an apple on the cover. The model in the artwork was revealed to be Nicole West. As with previous Aerosmith songs, the video also received huge attention. It starred actress Mils Kunis.

In January 2001 Aerosmith performed at the infamous Super Bowl halftime show. Produced by MTV, which was then a sister network of CBS, the halftime show also featured N Sync, Britney Spears, Nelly, Mary J. Blige, and Tremors featuring The Earthquake Horns. The show featured a back-and-forth medley between Aerosmith and N Sync. It showcased their new single 'Jaded' and also 'I Don't Want to Miss a Thing'. The show's finale was all of the performers singing Aerosmith's 'Walk This Way'. The Super Bowl this year was Baltimore Ravens vs New York Giants. Baltimore took the Super Bowl winning 34-7 on January 28th 2001. The game, and therefore the halftime show, was seen in the stadium by over 70,000 fans, and the estimated TV audience was 84.3 million viewers.

With 'Jaded' still high in the charts Aerosmith released their thirteenth studio album, *Just Push Play*, on March 6th 2001. It was recorded from April-December 2000 at various recording studios over the period, including The Boneyard and The Briar Patch, Long View Farms Studio, Ocean Way Studios, Sound Techniques, Village Recorders, Pearl White Studios, Whatinthewhatthe? Studios and The Studio in the Sunset Marquis. There were many songs that were recorded for the album but were eventually not used in the final cut; these included 'Ain't It True', 'Easy', 'Innocent Man', 'I Love You Down', 'Do You Wonder' and 'Sweet Due'. Also recorded and not used was 'Angel's Eye', which was used for the soundtrack to *Charlie's Angels*, while 'Face' and 'Won't Let You Down' were issued as bonus tracks on later pressings of the album.

Again, the album used outside collaborators contributing to the tracks. The final track listing was as follows: 'Beyond Beautiful' written by Steven Tyler, Joe Perry and Marti Frederiksen, 'Just Push Play' written by Steven Tyler, Mark Hudson and Steve Dudas, 'Jaded' written by Steven Tyler and

Marti Frederiksen, 'Fly Away From Here' written by Marti Frederiksen and Todd Chapman, 'Trip Hoppin' written by Steven Tyler, Joe Perry, Marti Frederiksen and Mark Hudson, 'Sunshine' written by Steven Tyler, Joe Perry and Marti Frederiksen, 'Under My Skin' written by Steven Tyler, Joe Perry, Marti Frederiksen and Mark Hudson, 'Luv Liee' written by Steven Tyler, Joe Perry, Marti Frederiksen and Mark Hudson, 'Outta Your Head' written by Steven Tyler, Joe Perry and Marti Frederiksen, 'Drop Dead Gorgeous' written by Steven Tyler, Joe Perry and Mark Hudson, 'Light Inside' written by Steven Tyler, Joe Perry and Marti Frederiksen and 'Avant Garden' written by Steven Tyler, Joe Perry, Marti Frederiksen and Mark Hudson. There was an international version that included 'Face/ Under My Skin (Reprise which starts at 3:38)' and also included the video for 'Jaded'. The Japanese version included 'Won't Let You Down' and 'I Don't Want to Miss a Thing'. The Japanese were also treated to a limited-edition version which included 'Just Push Play' as a Radio Remix, 'Same Old Song and Dance' recorded live from California Jam II '78, 'Draw the Line' again live from California Jam II '78, 'Chip Away the Stone' again live from California Jam II '78, 'Big Ten Inch Record' live from Texxas Jam '78 and 'Lord of the Thighs' again live from Texxas Jam '78.

Just Push Play was quickly certified platinum on the back of the success of 'Jaded', doing so within a month of its release. The album actually debuted straight in at number two on the Billboard 200, selling over 240,000 copies in its first week alone. Aerosmith were inducted to the Rock and Roll Hall of Fame soon after the album was released, in late March 2001, and in doing so became the only band to be inducted to the Hall of Fame with a song active in the charts, for 'Jaded'. Its subsequent singles, 'Fly Away from Here', 'Sunshine' and the title track 'Just Push Play', were not as successful as the lead but did gather airplay and also charted on the US Mainstream Rock Chart. The title track was also used in Dodge commercials and garnered significant exposure throughout the year. The album was nominated for three Grammy Awards in 2001: Best Rock Album, Best Rock Performance by a Duo or Group for 'Jaded', and Best Short Form Music Video for 'Fly Away From Here'.

In typical Aerosmith style the band started the Just Push Play Tour shortly after the album's release. It started in June 2001 and ran right through until February 2002, covering 77 concerts. The band Fuel was the support act for most of the tour, being replaced later by The Cult. The tour was a great success even though there were cancellations along the way; three were due to September 11 terrorist attacks; two of these were made up on the tour. There were a further eleven cancellations which were due to various illnesses of the band members.

The band kept a modern theme for the tour, in keeping with the album cover itself. There were many striking colour elements, particularly in the silver and white colours, and the stage had two large swirling staircases and a platform raised above which led to a very crowd-pleasing dramatic entrance for both Steven Tyler and Joe Perry at the beginning of the show. As most of the venues the band played at were huge stadiums, they also opted for a small stage in the rear of outdoor pavilions to be set up. As a result, half way through the concert they would perform a short three song set for those at the rear on the smaller stage. Steve Tyler jokingly referred to this section on the lawned area as the 'Back On The Grass' tour.

In response to the cancellations due to the September 11 attacks Aerosmith played the United We Stand: What More Can I Give benefit concert in aid of the victims of the terrorist attacks in New York. This was held at the RFK Stadium in Washington, D.C. on October 21, 2001. Many others performed during the event including Mariah Carey, James Brown, Al Green, Pink, Huey Lewis and Destiny's Child. Aerosmith couldn't fully commit to the show due to having another show on the same evening; however, they made the decision and agreed at the last minute. They played their set in the afternoon and performed four songs, then immediately flew to Indianapolis for a concert that same night.

The standard set list during the tour featured a wide variety of songs spanning their career and they made a conscious effort to vary it from night to night. The set list also featured at least half of the songs featured on *Just Push Play* as well as the usual concert staples spanning their career from the 1970s, 80s and 90s. The demand for the shows was incredible and many sold out immediately on release. The recent appearance at the Super Bowl, the induction into The Rock and Roll Hall of Fame and the huge hit 'Jaded' had pushed the album and their popularity sky high as a touring band. Steven Tyler had also performed the USA national anthem at the Indianapolis 500, and the team sponsored a car in the race; this again drew huge numbers in TV audience. As a result of the huge demand for tickets the band were forced to add dates through the autumn and winter. The tour became one of the highest grossing in 2001 with a reported $43,578,874; it had an attendance of over 937,600 fans. The band also played The Joint, a 2,000-seat venue within the Hard Rock Hotel and Casino. This show was recorded with parts released. This would form Aerosmith's fifth live album, a dual disc CD and DVD entitled *Rockin' the Joint* which was released later, in 2005.

During the tour Aerosmith had parts recorded for the VH1 series *Behind the Music*. This successful series profiled and interviewed a popular musical artist or group. It first began in 1997. The programme examines the beginning of a band or artist's career, their road to success and the hardships they may have encountered, while celebrating the success of whoever they are profiling on the episode. The Aerosmith VH1 special not only chronicled the band's history but also the band's current activities and touring, in this case the Just Push Play Tour. The episode on Aerosmith was one of the few *Behind the Music* specials to run for two hours in length; most were around 60-90 minutes. The special was aired in September 2002.

Also in 2002 another huge movie was about to be released for which Aerosmith contributed to the soundtrack. The album *Music From and Inspired by Spider-Man* was the soundtrack album for the film *Spider-Man*. The album also contains a portion of the film score which was by Danny Elfman, although a more complete album of Elfman's work was released as *Spider-Man: Original Motion Picture Score*. There were 21 tracks on the album, with Aerosmith contributing the 'Theme from Spiderman' at track 19 on the soundtrack. The singles released for the album were 'Hero' written by Chad Kroeger featuring Josey Scott, 'What We're All About' performed by Sum 41 and featuring Kerry King from Slayer and 'Bother' by Stone Sour and credited as Corey Taylor.

Continuing into 2002 Aerosmith made another appearance to a huge global audience. The FIFA World Cup 2002 was held in Korea and Japan. Aerosmith played at the official World Cup ceremony concert held at the Tokyo Stadium.

2002 was proving to be another huge year for Aerosmith. The past months had seen them play to incredible audiences around the world, both on tour and on TV, and the induction to the Rock and Roll Hall of Fame had encompassed and encapsulated them as a legendary outfit in rock and roll. The band again, in keeping with past strategies, looked at releasing an album to showcase the past hits, and the double disc they were now about to release would be a complete statement. It would contain at least twenty-eight of the band's biggest hits spanning their entire career up to this point in 2002. Oh Yeah!

Honkin' The Blues

The album *O, Yeah! Ultimate Aerosmith Hits* became a definitive statement for Aerosmith. It solidified them as a unique and truly remarkable rock outfit. The album, released by Columbia Records and Geffen Records, stood as a double-disc album showcasing 28 of the band's biggest hits in chronological order, spanning the band's entire career up to this point in 2002. Also included are two new songs: 'Girls of Summer' and 'Lay it Down', which the band recorded in Hawaii.

'Girls of Summer' was the only single released from the album, in August 2002. The track was written by Steven Tyler, Joe Perry and Marti Frederiksen in Hawaii, following the end of the Just Push Play Tour. The song is very laid back and utilised Pro Tools. The other track from these sessions, 'Bad Enough', was intended originally for the *Spider-Man* soundtrack, but this was replaced however with the Aerosmith cover of the Spider-Man theme song. It was then subsequently rewritten into another track present on *O Yeah!*, 'Lay It Down'. The single reached 25 on the US Mainstream Rock Tracks Chart and spawned the Girls of Summer Tour which was now in the planning. The song was nominated for a Grammy Award in 2003 in the category Best Rock Performance by a Duo or Group with Vocal. The video for the song, which was directed by David Meyers, was filmed in South Beach Miami. The three women appearing in the video are Jaime Pressly, Nichole Galicia, and Kim Smith.

The album itself went on to become certified double platinum. It was later rereleased in September 2013 as *The Essential Aerosmith* with a different album cover. The cover on the rerelease was a more standard profile of the band; the contents of the album however remained the same.

From August through to December 2002 Aerosmith embarked on a relatively short tour, by their standards, to promote the new compilation album. It would run for 51 shows. The Girls of Summer Tour covered North America and played in 41 amphitheatres with 10 arena shows, for a total of 51 shows. The tour was opened by Kid Rock and Run-DMC, which continued the trend of high-profile acts willing to open for them. Most support acts were usually up and coming acts that were in need of promotion. They would often be artists or bands that would not be able to fill the capacity of the stadium they were playing as they didn't yet have the following. With Aerosmith however even established large global acts were happy to support and open for them around the world, such was their status. This tour was one of the biggest events of Run-DMC's career, exposing them to large, live mainstream fanbases, generally unheard of in rap music. This was also the last major tour for Jam Master Jay. He was fatally shot this year, in October 2002, shortly after they had completed their opening performances on the first leg. Kid Rock also had a huge slot at the beginning of the show; he performed an exceptionally long set for an opening act which sometimes lasted for well over an hour at a time.

The stage setup was relatively simple, with ramps going out on the sides. They repeated the second stage performances during the shows once more; a B-stage for fans in the lawn, where they performed a three-song set of primarily 1970s classics during the middle of the show. The show started with a white curtain in front of the stage with Steven Tyler standing in silhouette on one of the monitors. The band usually adjusted their set list, but on most occasions opened the show with 'Toys in the Attic', playing behind a curtain until it came down when the band got into the song. They then continued through around 20 to 25 songs spanning their career. The track list was roughly 'Toys In The Attic', 'Back in the Saddle', 'Same Old Song And Dance', 'Girls of Summer', 'Sweet Emotion', 'What It Takes', 'Big Ten Inch Record', 'Dream On', 'Walking The Dog', 'I Don't Want To Miss A Thing', Last Child', Jaded', 'Pink', 'Stop Messin' Around', 'Lord of the Thighs',

'Cryin', 'Dude (Looks Like A Lady)', 'Draw the Line' and 'Walk This Way'. Other songs performed included 'Mama Kin', 'Love in an Elevator', 'Big Ten Inch Record', 'Monkey On My Back', and 'Janie's Got a Gun'. In addition, and to keep things interesting, they included a variety of lesser known songs and B-sides, which the band rotated heavily. During the encore, Kid Rock and Run-DMC joined Aerosmith for the final rendition of 'Walk This Way', celebrating the rejuvenation of the song's popularity. It also followed the collaborative nature of the track during the performance at Super Bowl XXXV and other high-profile events, as well as the re-uniting of Aerosmith and Run-DMC since they collaborated on the song back in 1986. The tour was deemed as usual to be a great success. The total gross income was reported to be $38,998,028 with a total attendance of 779,827.

Also in 2002 Aerosmith were honoured with an MTV Icon. MTV Icon was a series of annual television specials which was produced by the channel running from 2001 and 2004. Each show payed tribute to a musical artist or band selected as a cultural icon, in a format similar to the network's annual Video Music Awards and Movie Awards events. A live audience of musicians, celebrities and fans would view a biographical film depicting the career of that year's chosen icon, interspersed with celebrity introductions and live performances of popular artists playing cover versions of the icon's songs. The iconic artist would then accept an award and perform a live set of their own at the close of the show. The series celebrated Janet Jackson in 2001 and Aerosmith in 2002. Later participants of the award were Metallica in 2003, and The Cure in 2004. The event began with the previous year's icon, Janet Jackson, delivering a testimonial about the band. It featured performances by The X-Ecutioners, Nelly, Ja Rule, DJ Clue, Sum 41, Pink, Shakira, Kid Rock, Train, and Papa Roach. The show concluded with Aerosmith themselves performing a five-song set: 'Movin' Out', 'Toys in the Attic', 'Cryin', 'Girls of Summer' and 'Train Kept A-Rollin'.

Moving into 2003, Aerosmith now planned an album to take them back to their roots in blues. They performed from August onwards in The Rocksimus Maximus Tour/World Domination Tour, which was a North American concert tour co-headlined by

Aerosmith and Kiss. The tour was actually referred to as the World Domination Tour by Kiss and was called the Rocksimus Maximus Tour by Aerosmith. To make things even more complicated it was also known as the 'AeroKiss Tour' incorporating the names of both headlining bands. The tour took place during the second half of 2003, performing at amphitheatres across the United States in late summer and early autumn and then on to arenas in late autumn and early winter. There were 59 shows played from August through to December. The tour reportedly earned in excess of $64 million in 2003. Kiss had already toured, prior to joining Aerosmith, across Australia and Japan, before joining up for the North America leg. Once Kiss had completed their show Aerosmith took to the stage with a concert that consisted of a mix of old and newer material, including a three-song blues set during the middle of the show. This was in connection to the forthcoming blues tracks to be featured on their then-upcoming album *Honkin' on Bobo*. The stage design also changed for this section of the show. Aerosmith also played several classic 'deep cuts' from the 1970s that they hadn't played in years, including 'Adam's Apple' and 'Nobody's Fault' among others.

In March 2004 Aerosmith released their fourteenth studio album, *Honkin' on Bobo*. It was recorded throughout 2003. The album, put out by Columbia Records, includes 11 covers of blues songs from the 1950s and 1960s, with one new song entitled 'The Grind'. The album is a return to basics for the band and is in some ways a tribute to Aerosmith's earliest influences, and it showcases a rawer sound, reminiscent of their 1970s work, certainly in comparison to their more recent commercial efforts. Showcasing this return and in pursuit of getting the sound they wanted the band once more employed producer Jack Douglas, who was Aerosmith's producer on a vast majority of their 1970s releases. *Honkin' On Bobo* was recorded in Joe Perry's ranch near Boston, with the band reportedly playing only when they were in a good mood. The unusual title for the album came from Steven Tyler, who heard the phrase somewhere, and the band found it funny. They felt the phrase sounded a bit jazzy so it worked and was agreed. There is a big emphasis on harmonica, performed by Steven Tyler, which incorporates the early blues sound. The tracks included a cover of Little Walter's 'Temperature' which was played on an episode of the House of Blues Radio Hour in tribute to the harmonica. A harmonica keychain was included with the limited-edition version that was released. Many critics praised the album and cited it as the return of Aerosmith.

After the sessions the band chose the following recordings to be included on the album: 'Road Runner', a Bo Diddley cover written by Ellas McDaniel a.k.a. Bo Diddley, 'Shame, Shame, Shame', originally sung by Smiley Lewis, written by Ruby Fisher and Kenyon Hopkins, 'Eyesight to the Blind', a Sonny Boy Williamson II cover written by Sonny Boy Williamson II, 'Baby, Please Don't Go', a Big Joe Williams cover, written by Joe Williams, 'Never Loved a Girl', an Aretha Franklin cover written by Ronny Shannon, 'Back Back Train', a Mississippi Fred McDowell cover, written by Fred McDowell, 'You Gotta Move', a Mississippi Fred McDowell cover written by Rev. Gary Davis and Fred McDowell, 'The Grind' written by Steven Tyler, Joe Perry and Marti Frederiksen, 'I'm Ready', a Muddy Waters cover written by Willie Dixon, 'Temperature', a Little Walter cover written by Joel Michael Cohen and Walter Jacobs, 'Stop Messin' Around', a Fleetwood Mac cover written by Clifford Adams and Peter Green and 'Jesus is on the Main Line', a Mississippi Fred McDowell cover, a traditional arrangement by F. McDowell.

The only single to be released from the album was 'Baby, Please Don't Go', which was a traditional blues song that was popularised by Delta blues musician Big Joe Williams in 1935. Many cover versions of the song followed over the years, making it one of the most played, arranged, and rearranged pieces in blues history. The track reached number seven on the Mainstream Rock Tracks Chart. A music video, directed by Mark Haefeli, was produced to promote the single. After the release the song was quickly added to the concert set lists and has become a staple of the band's concert repertoire. *Honkin' on Bobo* was a return to the band's roots and also included recording the album in live sessions. The album sold over 160,000 copies in its first week, reaching number five on the Billboard 200. It went on to be certified gold by the Recording Industry Association of America.

In promotion of the record and in keeping with the return to a roots sound Aerosmith embarked on the Honkin' on Bobo Tour to support their new album. The tour sent the band to small venues throughout North America as well as Japan, starting on March 11th 2004 and concluding on July 25th 2004. The tour was unique and a departure from the huge venues they had played in the past. Here they played in smaller arenas and in smaller markets in the south and midwest of the US. Additionally, the set list varied widely from show to show, but was generally no longer than 20 songs, and featured several of their classics, as well as new bluesy tunes from *Honkin' on Bobo* including 'Baby, Please Don't Go', 'Road Runner', 'Stop Messin' Around', and 'Never Loved a Girl'. Rock band Cheap Trick was the opening act for the majority of the tour. The stage setup was meant to imitate an old blues club, and was purposely toned down from the huge theatre of past Aerosmith shows, more in keeping with the return to grass roots and blues that the band used to play. They even had neon signs in the back and an intentionally relatively simple stage. There was also a catwalk, a format which would continue on subsequent Aerosmith tours. The DVD release, *You Gotta Move,* became the band's first live video compilation since 1987 and was culled primarily from the Orlando performance on the tour. This was originally aired as an A&E television special. The DVD was released in late 2004.

Moving into 2005, Steven Tyler and Joe Perry moved for a short time into separate projects. Steven Tyler appeared in the movie *Be Cool* with the band as they made a cameo appearance while Joe Perry himself released his self-titled debut album. *Joe Perry* was his first solo album, released on May 3rd 2005 on Sony BMG. It was also his first without The Joe Perry Project. The album was also released as a standard CD and a dual disc. Joe Perry performed all guitars, bass, keyboards and vocals on all 13 tracks on the record, leaving only the drums and percussion to the album's co-producer, Paul Caruso. The album also contains a cover of 'The Crystal Ship' which was performed by The Doors. A year later in 2006 at the Grammy Awards, Joe Perry was nominated for Best Rock Instrumental Performance for the track 'Mercy'.

The band next released another live album, this time entitled *Rockin' the Joint.* It was released on October 25, 2005. The album was recorded in January 2002 in The Joint at the Hard Rock Hotel in Las Vegas, and consists of Aerosmith classics and more recent songs performed live. The CD contained 12 tracks with the DVD showcasing four: 'No More No More', 'Dream On', 'Draw the Line' and 'Sweet Emotion'. The Japanese version also contained 'Toys in the Attic' and 'Livin' on the Edge'.

Starting on October 30th 2005 Aerosmith started another tour in support of *Rockin' the Joint.* The Rockin' the Joint Tour was a North American concert tour that ran from 2005–2006. The first leg ran from October 30 through to February 24 hitting most major US markets; shows on this leg were opened by Lenny Kravitz. The second leg was scheduled to run from March to April 2006, reaching some of the smaller US markets and opened by veteran band Cheap Trick. It was, however, cut short when Steven Tyler required throat surgery. Lenny Kravitz had always been a friend of Aerosmith and even ran a competition for his fans to travel on his tour bus. Steven Tyler joined Lenny for some of these trips, making it even more special for fans. The tour wasn't without its issues, with Steven Tyler requiring throat surgery, so it was disrupted throughout. Lenny himself also had some major personal news when, on October 29th 2005, he was told his father had died after a short fight with leukaemia; the next night, on October 30th when Lenny was scheduled to perform ahead of Aerosmith, he announced the news to the crowd, and dedicated his signature song 'Let Love Rule' to his father during the performance.

Steven Tyler managed to perform through his throat issues but widespread reports were circulating around regarding the issue and many concerts were shorter than expected for fans. The initial set list had dropped and many fans were venting frustration at the relatively short sets when they had paid a high price for tickets. The ticket prices themselves were as high as $150 and even the cheaper seats were in excess of $85. The set list issue was a key focus on the tour and was heavily criticised: the set list the band played initially started at around 20 songs but this was noticeably reduced to around 16 songs and it was evident this was done to sustain the tour to completion; sadly, though, this didn't happen, even though the band tried in vain to continue. It left many fans feeling that they were not getting their money's worth out of the concerts. An announcement was made on March 22nd 2006 that Steven Tyler needed throat surgery and thus the remaining dates of the tour were cancelled. The band themselves were put on hiatus indefinitely until Steven Tyler fully recovered.

For the shows the band employed a unique stage setup which featured two long catwalks, extending slightly diagonally from the main stage. This allowed the band more flexibility in working the crowd, and giving all seats a better view of the band members while they were performing. The band mixed up their set list heavily, starting out the tour with their main hits, and eventually including rarities like 'Walkin' the Dog', 'S.O.S. (Too Bad)', and the first live performance of 'Kings and Queens' in more than a decade. The show also featured Joe Perry performing as the lead singer and guitarist on his solo hit 'Shakin' My Cage.' Joey Kramer's son filled in for about 2-4 songs at some of the earlier shows, as his dad's shoulder healed from a previous injury.

There were initially 61 dates scheduled for the tour and 44 actually played. Within these 44 concerts there were the shorter set lists as Steven Tyler attempted to persevere despite his throat issues. As the tour entered March 2006 all remaining shows were cancelled. Despite the setback the tour was again a huge success financially for the band and all of the dates that went ahead were sold out.

Steven Tyler now needed time to recover, but this wouldn't take long. Aerosmith were always one thing: an incredible live touring band, and this was always their primary focus - to get back on the circuit. They loved the road and the live performance, for them it was what rock and roll was all about. They now planned a tour once more and this time they partnered it alongside another rocking Crüe.

The Route of All Evil

Aerosmith worked on new tracks for a planned new album as they entered 2006. They also teamed up with fellow rockers Mötley Crüe for a planned joint tour together. Firstly, however, they performed a small tester. On July 4th 2006 Steven Tyler and Joe Perry teamed up with the Boston Pops Orchestra for the annual July 4th concert. It was the first time Steven had performed since his throat surgery, and all went well, with no major issues. It signalled his return and the plans went ahead for the new tour. The Route of all Evil Tour ran from September 2006 through to December. There were 40 shows which combined both Aerosmith and Mötley Crüe, five with Aerosmith only and five with Mötley Crüe only.

Shortly into the tour Aerosmith released another compilation album titled *Devil's Got a New Disguise* or *The Very Best of Aerosmith* as it was titled in the UK. The album was released a month into the tour on October 17, 2006. It was intended to complete Aerosmith's contract with Sony Music/Columbia Records until the release of a new studio album; however, this did not happen for quite a few years, in fact not until *Music from Another Dimension!* which was finally released in November 2012.

The band and the new material they were working on had numerous problems and setbacks. There was Steven Tyler requiring throat surgery from March 2006 and then time to recover fully, bassist Tom Hamilton having treatment for throat cancer and also needing time for recovery, and there was issues again with their record company. As a result, the band simply didn't have the time to complete a new album full of new material, so they opted instead to release another compilation album. The album features 18 Aerosmith hits but presented in the single-remix versions; again it covers their illustrious career. To make it appealing to hard-core fans as much as new recruits the band put two new tracks onto the album: the title track, 'Devil's Got a New Disguise', and 'Sedona Sunrise'. 'Devil's Got a New Disguise' was a track that was taken from outtakes from the *Pump* sessions; the song had a different name then, however. It was initially called 'Susie Q' and had unfinished lyrics; later, during 1992's *Get a Grip* sessions its title changed to 'Devil's Got a New Disguise'. The song was co-written by Diane Warren and for the 2006 version a few lines of the lyrics were changed. The song when released was another good hit for Aerosmith and received plenty of airplay; it peaked at number 15 on the Mainstream Rock Tracks Chart. 'Sedona Sunrise' was again taken from *Pump* sessions, this time co-written by Jim Vallance. The European edition of the album was released on 30 October 2006 and it features five tracks which are different from the American version. These tracks are: 'Amazing', 'Angel', 'Falling in Love (Is Hard on the Knees)', 'Pink', and 'The Other Side'. The tracks that were on the American edition of the album but are not on the European edition of the album are: 'Back in the Saddle', 'Last Child', 'Mama Kin', 'Rag Doll' and 'What It Takes'.

The Route of all Evil Tour was a tour in reality to keep the momentum going for both bands as they prepared new albums. Aerosmith also had the compilation album to support and of course it was a great show to highlight their back catalogue. Mötley Crüe themselves had also released a compilation album of their own; their last studio album was in 2000 titled *New Tattoo*. After the tour reached the end of November it started the second leg, which had an additional ten arena dates. Half of these featured Aerosmith only. Additionally, Mötley Crüe performed several solo shows at smaller venues during the course of the tour, during days off. American singer-songwriter and record producer Lennon Murphy also performed on some of the dates with both bands.

With this tour being the first continuous set of dates since Steven Tyler had undergone throat surgery there were naturally some concerns about whether his voice would hold out for the concerts. It did and there were no issues. Another concern was over exposure. Aerosmith had toured almost continuously over the past few years and there was a fear that the venues would not sell as well as they normally would. Teaming up with another band to make a rock spectacle was therefore a good strategy. The ticket prices were also again high with some as much as $150 for good seats. Despite this most shows were very well attended or sold out completely; the figures therefore were impressive and reported to be very high. The tour was only 40 shows, which by Aerosmith standards was pretty low, but despite this it was still placed as one of the highest-grossing tours of 2006. The tour earned a reported $36 million. Also, fans and the press alike praised the tour and the performances; most praise was directed naturally towards Aerosmith, who were far superior.

Mötley Crüe's stage setup featured a wide range of props and a full pyrotechnics display. Aerosmith's stage setup featured a 70-foot-long catwalk and bright lighting. It also featured a sit-down acoustic performance during which fake snow fell. There was a huge video screen and the usual curtain that fell when the band started the concert. Within the set they added a cover of the song 'Dirty Water' which was played at both shows in their hometown of Boston, to pay homage to their city. The version the band played didn't waiver too much and stayed true to The Standells' original recording. The Mansfield crowd reacted to the song with tremendous energy and excitement. Tom Hamilton, who had been out of the line-up for most of the tour due to his recovery from throat cancer, returned briefly to play 'Sweet Emotion' at the first Boston show. He would later return as the sole bassist at the very next tour date, on December 1, 2006, in Detroit. Also, at the show on October 2, 2006 in Toronto it was Tommy Lee's birthday, and Lee joined Aerosmith to play 'Last Child' on drums. He previously asked Steven Tyler to play this particular song as a birthday gift.

The set list throughout the tour ranged anywhere from 12 to 17 songs, with most shows amounting to around 13; however, many of the east and west coast shows featured 14 or 15 songs. The set included an overwhelming majority of classics from their 1970s period, as well as several bluesy numbers in keeping with their last album, and many fused into extended jams. Although the set list varied there were songs that they played at every show. These staples were 'Cryin', 'Stop Messin' Around', 'Seasons of Wither' (with 'Hangman Jury' as an intro occasionally), 'Sweet Emotion', 'Draw the Line' and 'Walk This Way'. Other songs played included 'Toys in the Attic', 'Eat the Rich', 'Love in an Elevator', 'Jaded', 'Mama Kin', 'S.O.S. (Too Bad)', 'Dude (Looks Like a Lady)', 'Walkin' the Dog', 'Big Ten Inch Record', 'Baby, Please Don't Go', 'What It Takes', 'Rag Doll', 'Dream On', 'Back in the Saddle', 'Last Child', 'No More No More', 'Lord of the Thighs', 'Pink', 'Rattlesnake Shake', 'Train Kept A-Rollin', 'Dirty Water', 'One Way Street', 'Livin' on the Edge' and 'Devil's Got a New Disguise'. There were also a couple of surprises with rare performances of 'Kings and Queens' and 'Chip Away the Stone'. The band had two songs typically as encores which were the crowd favourites of 'Love in an Elevator' and 'Walk This Way'.

Entering 2007 Aerosmith announced a new world tour. Even though they had toured consistently this would be in fact their first for eight years outside of North America and Japan, since The Nine Lives Tour. In some territories it was the first for fourteen years since the Get a Grip Tour. It was simply named Aerosmith World Tour 2007 or The Tour Heard Round the World. It commenced in early 2007 in South America, where the band performed to huge stadiums, and all sold out, such was their everlasting live popularity.

The tour started in Sao Paulo, Brazil at the Estadio do Morumbi on April 12th before moving to Argentina on the 15th. There were then three shows in Mexico and two in the USA in Las Vegas on April 28th and New York on May 2nd. Two shows in Asia followed at United Arab Emirates in Dubai on May 31st before a show in Bangalore in India. The European leg commenced on June 6th 2007 in Denmark at Essex Park Randers. It then travelled through Sweden, Germany, France, Belgium and England.

The tour showcased again a majority of crowd favourites being played; this was in keeping with the recent release of the compilation album *Devil's Got a New Disguise*. The set list comprised of: 'Love in an Elevator', 'Same Old Song and Dance', 'Cryin', 'Eat the Rich' 'Jaded','I Don't Want to Miss a Thing', 'What It Takes', 'Baby, Please Don't Go', 'Hangman Jury', 'Seasons of Wither', 'S.O.S. (Too Bad)', 'Dream On', 'Livin' on the Edge', 'Stop Messin' Around', 'Sweet Emotion', 'Draw the Line' and 'Walk This Way'.

Moving into summer, the band performed throughout Europe and Asia, also making appearances at numerous major festivals. The band also played a select few concerts in Canada and California at the end of July. The July 21st concert Aerosmith performed at Prince Edward Island was the largest in that province's history. In September 2007, the band performed eight dates in north-eastern America, these shows being opened by Joan Jett.

While in England the band performed at London's Hard Rock Cafe in February 2007 and also at Hyde Park as part of the Hyde Park Calling festival sponsored by Hard Rock Café in June. It was Aerosmith's first concert in the United Kingdom for eight years, and featured Peter Gabriel and the recently reformed Crowded House as joint headliners for the first day of the festival. Sunday became an 'Aerosmith family' event when they headlined the main stage. It was opened by The Micki Free Electric Blues, then Arckid, which was a band featuring Steve Tyler's son-in-law. Chris Cornell played the main stage before Aerosmith made their appearance. TAB the Band played fourth on the bill on the second stage featuring Joe Perry's two sons. Many people saw the event as unbalanced, with most commercially successful bands playing on the Sunday; they were correct is raising this - Aerosmith in particular had sold more albums and toured to more fans than both of Saturday's headline bands put together. As it was Sunday Aerosmith were forced to finish at 10.30 pm due to the curfew laws, and the police forced them to leave. The encore was the usual 'Walk this Way' and this time featured Darryl McDaniels AKA 'DMC'. This was the first time a member of Run-DMC had performed with Aerosmith since their 2002 tour, five years previously.

The tour continued in Ireland, then Germany, the Netherlands, Latvia, Estonia, Finland and Russia where the band played two shows in St Petersburg and Moscow. The band returned to North America for some festival dates in July starting in Ontario at Sarnio Bayfest. The festival is an annual music festival in Centennial Park - downtown Sarnia, Ontario, Canada, which takes place in July each year. Since 1999, Rogers Bayfest has grown from attracting a few thousand visitors to approximately 100,000. The festival is run by Bayfest Festival of Performing Arts, a non-profit charitable organisation. Bayfest involves and benefits a number of charities and capitalises on the hometown feeling and the festival environment. Aerosmith performed at the event on July 19th 2007. Two days later they performed the record-breaking Blast at the Beach festival held in Prince Edward Island in Canada and then onto Mid State Fair at Paso Rhodes in California. The California Mid-State Fair is held annually and runs for 12 days at the end of July. Aerosmith headlined the event on July 25th 2007. On July 27th they played at Konocti Harbour Resort and music venue in Kelseyville, California. The venue is in a stunning location situated at the base of Mount Konocti on the south shore of Clear Lake, the largest freshwater lake interior to California.

The tour concluded in Hawaii with a private concert. They did plan a public show which was scheduled for Maui but this was cancelled for logistical reasons. Unfortunately, this led to a class action lawsuit against the band. Later in April 2009 they agreed to compensate all ticket buyers with a free ticket to a rescheduled Maui show to be held on October 20, 2009. This also included reimbursements of all out-of-pocket expenses related to the show. The band performed in a total of 19 countries and the tour was another major success, yet again making them one of highest grossing touring acts of 2007.

On November 1, 2007, the band entered the studio to work on the final studio album of their current contract with Sony. At the time, it was believed that the album would include some songs that didn't make previous albums and had not as yet been released. This was a growing list, such was the band's output. The tracks were initially to be rerecorded for inclusion as well as brand new material that they were writing alongside their now usual collaborators. While this was in the planning stages the band started working closely with gaming once more. Gaming was an area that was becoming increasingly lucrative for bands financially and good for their overall kudos and popularity. Any band with longevity that was still popular could capitalise and reach new audiences in this growing market which was turning into a huge monster in its own right. Years before it was only albums, singles and videos that really promoted a band, and they would then tour and build upon this. More recently blockbuster movies started to integrate soundtracks and singles, the singles and albums promoting the movie and the movie promoting the singles and albums. If a movie and a combined album with singles and videos worked, then the results could be absolutely huge, everything working together to create a massive marketing campaign and all under one roof; if this was under the same record/movie company then the results would be incredible and the popularity of the movie and any band associated with it would smash through once again.

Aerosmith had been very successful in crossing over into these areas of cross media, and now gaming was the next big avenue to walk into. Of all bands out there they fitted this more than any other: they were Rock Royalty, Rock Gods; Guitar Heroes.

Heroes of Rock

The *Guitar Hero* series had been around for some time and had become extremely popular. The series was first published in 2005 by RedOctane and Harmonix, and was distributed by Activision. The popular game has players use a guitar-shaped game controller to simulate playing lead guitar, bass guitar, and rhythm guitar across numerous rock music songs. The series had grown and expanded rapidly and now Aerosmith were in line to become the first band to have their own dedicated version of the game.

The game was released on the PlayStation 3, Wii and Xbox 360 consoles. It was released on June 26th 2008 in Europe and on June 29th 2008 in North America, in August in Australia and in October in Japan. *Guitar Hero: Aerosmith* sold as both a bundle with a specially designed guitar controller as well as a game-only package. The game was a basic expansion of the *Guitar Hero* series but was the first game in the series to primarily focus on the work of one rock band, with Aerosmith songs comprising approximately 70% of the soundtrack; the remaining songs are from bands that have been influenced by or have opened for Aerosmith. The single player career mode allows the player to follow the history of the band through several real-world-inspired venues. Each venue gets bigger as the stages are passed through playing various Aerosmith songs. The game is also interspersed with interviews from the band members about their past. Aerosmith re-recorded four songs especially for the game, and they also participated in a motion capture session to create their in-game appearances to make it as realistic as possible.

Activision released Aerosmith's 'Dream On' to the Xbox Live Marketplace and the PlayStation Store as a free *Guitar Hero*

III: Legends of Rock downloadable song. The free download was available from February 16–18, 2008. It was then removed when the game was eventually released. Aerosmith themselves promoted the game with their appearance at the Hard Rock Cafe in New York City on June 27th 2008 where they took questions and tried out the game. The soundtrack itself was comprised of 41 songs; out of this 30 are playable during career mode and another 11 songs are unlockable in the vault. Twenty-nine of the songs are from Aerosmith themselves, with the rest from bands that have been inspired by them. The songs themselves are taken directly from master recordings with four re-recorded especially for the game itself. They are also four covers by Wavegroup Sound and Steve Ouimette.

On September 4th 2008 Steven Tyler appeared on VH1 Classic Radio and announced that Aerosmith intended to enter the studio at the end of September 2008 to complete the band's fifteenth studio album now that they had completed working on the video game. He also announced a new tour which was in the making, to commence in the US in June 2009. The new album at this point was still unnamed. Although these were good plans the fact that the band were planning the tour meant that the album was again put on hold, as they simply did not have time. They was also an injury to the knee of Joe Perry and he needed time for recovery. They announced, moving into 2009, that the album would be produced by the famed Brendan O'Brien and that the album would likely be recorded live, like their earlier records.

Brendan O'Brien had an impressive career to date and it's no wonder Aerosmith wanted him to produce their new album. He had worked with such artists as Pearl Jam, Bob Dylan, Neil Young, Bruce Springsteen, AC/DC, Red Hot Chili Peppers, Rage Against the Machine and The Black Crowes, amongst many others. In the mid-1990s he became vice president of Epic Records and the Epic imprint 57 Records. He also played a Hammond organ for Bob Dylan's appearance on *MTV Unplugged* and also toured as a musician; in 1995 he joined Pearl Jam and Neil Young on keyboard for the Mirror Ball tour which toured across Europe. Further forward he went on to win a Grammy Award for Best Rock Album for his work on Bruce Springsteen's *The Rising* in 2002 and he went on to be awarded a Grammy Award for Producer of the Year for Non-Classical. To date, fourteen of the albums O'Brien has produced have reached number one in the US on the Billboard 200 chart.

The tour itself commenced in June 2009 and resulted in the album being put on hold until it was at least completed. The tour featured ZZ Top as the support act for most of the shows. Unfortunately the tour was again met with numerous setbacks along the way. ZZ Top played a typical set list, spanning their career, of around 13 songs, and the set lasted for around an hour. Aerosmith's set list comprised of 'Train Kept A Rollin', 'Cryin', 'Love In An Elevator', 'Jaded', 'Dream On', 'Combination', 'Toys In The Attic', 'Uncle Salty', 'Adam's Apple', 'Walk This Way', 'Big Ten Inch Record', 'Sweet Emotion', 'No More No More', 'Round And Round' and 'Livin' On The Edge'. The encores were typically 'Dirty Water' and 'Come Together'. The set list, as with most Aerosmith tours, differed from time to time but for this tour that was the basic set list.

With the tour originally intended to promote the release of Aerosmith's new album, which the band had hoped to complete before the tour, it would have been a worthy collaboration with *Guitar Hero* for a new type of spectacle for the band. However, the setbacks were again in place for Aerosmith as they prepared and indeed commenced the tour itself. This included surgery to repair Joe Perry's knee and Steven Tyler suffering pneumonia, which prevented the album from being completed before the tour. Brad Whitford was also recovering from surgery and subsequently missed the first seven dates of the tour; he returned in mid-July.

The tour was named The Aerosmith/ZZ Top Tour but it was also referred to as the A to Z Tour or Guitar Hero: Aerosmith Tour. The tour started on June 10th 2009 and basically carried on through until it had to be cancelled unexpectedly due to shoulder injuries sustained by Steven Tyler. For the first seven dates of the tour, Aerosmith played the entire *Toys in the Attic* album at every show, with the exception of the last track, 'You See Me Crying'; however this was rectified when on June 26, 2009, while in Wantagh, New York's Jones Beach Theatre, Aerosmith did indeed play 'You See Me Crying', which was the first time in the band's history. This meant that for the first time every song on *Toys in the Attic* was played. It was also the first time that they played 'Round and Round' live. There was also a segment in the show where Joe Perry played against the animated version of himself in the *Guitar Hero: Aerosmith* video game. Promoting the game further it also featured a select one or two fans at each show playing a song from *Guitar Hero: Aerosmith* live onstage before the concert.

Several dates were cancelled mid-tour after Steven Tyler injured his leg in Uncasville, Connecticut. Additionally, guitarist Brad Whitford and bassist Tom Hamilton had to sit out several of the dates due to injuries or surgeries; Whitford and Hamilton had substitutes perform in their places. Aerosmith were forced to cancel the rest of the tour completely when Steven Tyler fell off the stage in Sturgis, South Dakota. Later, when he had recovered, the band played three more shows in October and November.

When Aerosmith resumed their tour, on July 15th in Atlanta, Brad Whitford re-joined the fold after recovering from his surgery; however, bassist Tom Hamilton had to again temporarily depart the tour in order to recover from non-invasive surgery, his spot being filled by David Hull until he recovered. Further problems lay ahead however during the concert on August 5th in Sturgis, South Dakota. The concert suffered a sound failure and was temporarily suspended, so Steven Tyler decided to entertain fans as technicians repaired the outage; but unfortunately he lost his footing and fell from the catwalk. He suffered head, neck, and shoulder injuries and had to be flown to a hospital in Rapid City. Naturally the rest of the Sturgis show was cancelled and the band had no choice but to cancel the rest of the tour altogether to allow him a full recovery.

Moving on to October, after Steven Tyler had recovered, two shows were played in Hawaii, with one in Maui and the other in Honolulu. Also in October Joe Perry completed work on his fifth solo album, titled *Have Guitar, Will Travel*. The album was released on October 6th 2009 on Roman Records. In addition to Joe Perry on lead guitar and vocals the album also features German vocalist Hagen Grohe, Joe Perry Project bassist David Hull, pianist Willie Alexander, organ player Paul Santo, and three drummers: Marty Richards, Ben Tileston and Scott Meeder. It was actually

Joe Perry's wife, Billie Perry, who discovered vocalist Hagen Grohe on YouTube after hearing about Journey discovering their vocalist Arnel Pineda in a similar manner. Joe Perry felt strongly that Steven Tyler was to blame for the aborted Aerosmith album so decided to travel south in the US to meet with Brendan O'Brien and play the new material. The song 'Do You Wonder' was originally intended for *Push Play* but remained unfinished. This was then intended for the next Aerosmith album but when it became postponed producer Brendan O'Brien commented on how much he loved the song. As a result, Joe Perry decided to push for it to be included in his own album. His wife Billie Perry wrote the lyrics to the track.

Joe Perry said that one of reasons he still kept releasing solo albums was because he didn't have to answer to anybody and he could more or less do what he wanted. The album's first single was 'We've Got a Long Way to Go'.

Later, in February 2010, *Have Guitar, Will Travel* received its UK release alongside issue 142 of *Classic Rock* magazine. The issue was a good piece of marketing for the album and featured an exclusive interview with Aerosmith and a 'track-by-track' interview with Joe Perry about the album. It's also a significant album as the background to it stemmed from when Steven Tyler had his accident and was again in recovery forcing the cancellation of the tour. The album was initially designed by Joe Perry to include some of the biggest musicians in rock music contributing to it - he originally planned to contact various notable figures to make guest appearances on the record, the likes of Jimmy Page, Slash, Scott Weiland, Robin Zander - but in the end he decided against it.

Drummer Joey Kramer also released his autobiography entitled *Hit Hard* in October 2009.

The first show the band played in Maui was played as part of the aforementioned legal settlement after the band was sued for cancelling a performance there in 2007. In November the band continued performing and played at the 2009 Abu Dhabi Grand Prix in the United Arab Emirates. There were heavily reported arguments around this time between Steven Tyler and Joe Perry, as their relationship had gone downhill after Steven Tyler's injury when he fell from the stage.

There was a planned tour of South America at the end of 2009 but as Joe Perry was pursuing his own solo project Steven Tyler did the same. He pulled out of the tour. Joe Perry himself began touring the US at the end of 2009, and Japan and the UK early in 2010. The rumours continued to circulate at this point that Steven Tyler was going to leave the band and was to be replaced by another singer, and in November 2009, Joe Perry stated that Steven Tyler had not been in contact with the band and could be on the verge of quitting Aerosmith. He then stated that the rest of the group was looking for a new singer to work with. It was also reported that singer Lenny Kravitz had been approached for Steven Tyler's position; naturally Lenny declined.

Even though these rumours were circulating around, Steven Tyler and Joe Perry joined each other onstage on November 10th 2009 at the Fillmore New York at Irving Plaza, performing 'Walk This Way' together. Steven Tyler reportedly announced to the crowd that he in fact was not quitting Aerosmith. Shortly afterwards it was reported that he had entered a rehabilitation facility to manage his addiction to painkillers, brought on by injuries to his knees, legs, and feet, which had resulted from years of performing. In his statement he said that he was grateful for the support he was receiving, was committed to getting things taken care of, and was eager to get back on stage and in the recording studio with his bandmates. Despite this, as 2010 came around Joe Perry again confirmed the band were about to audition for a new singer to replace Steven Tyler, stating that the surgery to his legs would take him out of the picture for up to a year and a half, and in the meantime, the rest of the band wanted to continue performing. He also said that the band would be willing to continue working with Tyler in the future if the singer wanted to. Steven Tyler, through his attorney, sent the band and its manager a 'cease and desist' letter and threatened further legal action against both if the band did not discontinue this effort to replace him.

Aerosmith even from the very start of their career were beautifully unpredictable, and this was no different: they had been splitting up essentially for nearly 40 years and always ended up back on stage. Here it was the same, as they agreed to headline one of the biggest rock festivals in the UK in mid tour. It seemed once again that despite the rumours they would hit the road once more for a huge sell out world tour. The tour was confirmed and would start in May 2010.

The last tour that Aerosmith embarked upon, with ZZ Top, was beset with issues from the start, mainly surrounding illnesses and accidents. It ended after just the one leg. Of the planned tour itself 28 shows were cancelled including the actual show where Steven Tyler fell from the stage and injured himself. There were four post-tour shows when he eventually recovered, before various solo projects took hold. The band clearly wanted to make amends for this and were keen once more to hit the road on a worldwide scale. This time they planned 42 shows covering three legs, and they were determined that all would take place without any issues. They were 'Cocked Locked and Ready to Rock'.

Rocking Into Another Dimension

The Cocked, Locked, Ready to Rock Tour included concerts for South America and Europe, which made it the first time the band had played those territories since 2007. Just before the tour commenced, the band announced that the lead singer would be Steven Tyler, so despite all the rumours there was no change. During the second half of summer, the band toured North America. The tour included a headlining show at Download Festival in UK, playing the festival's venue at Donington Park, the first time they had headlined the festival in 16 years. It had also been 16 years since they had performed in Venezuela, Chile, Costa Rica, and Romania, which again were planned areas for concerts. The tour also planned for Aerosmith to perform in Peru and Greece for the first time in their career. North America in particular was cited as including many locations which they had missed due to the cancellation of dates on their prior Guitar Hero: Aerosmith Tour in 2009. A total of 18 countries were scheduled.

The set list was scheduled for around 16 to 20 songs at each show and they planned it to span their career. There was also the inclusion of a drum solo by Joey Kramer during the middle of the set, and at most concerts Joe Perry performed a duel against the *Guitar Hero: Aerosmith* version of himself, as in the previous year's Guitar Hero: Aerosmith Tour, before performing a song in which he sang lead vocals; this was either 'Stop Messin' Around', 'Red House' or 'Combination'.

The tour started the first leg on May 17th 2010 at Caracas Venezuela at the 20,000 capacity Poliedro de Caracas Arena. It then moved on to Columbia, Peru, Chile, two shows in Brazil and Costa Rica which concluded the South American leg on June 1st

2010. There were no issues during this section and all were sold out. The second leg commenced in Europe on June 10th with a concert at The Sweden Rock Festival at Solvesborg. At this year's event were also Guns N Roses, Billy Idol, Gary Moore and Slayer amongst many others. The event this year ran from June 9th through to June 12th with Aerosmith headlining the festival. Three days later on June 13th Aerosmith headlined Download at Donington Park, England. Download has risen to become the most popular British summer rock and heavy metal festival, and it has gone on to showcase some of the genre's biggest names, including Saxon, Black Sabbath, Slipknot, Metallica, Iron Maiden, Korn, Soundgarden, Motörhead, AC/DC, Def Leppard, Kiss, Judas Priest, Status Quo, Mötley Crüe, Journey, ZZ Top, Whitesnake, Thin Lizzy, Faith No More and Guns N Roses. Aerosmith took to the stage as headliners on the Maurice Jones Mainstage amidst torrential heavy rain that had reduced the hundreds of thousands of spectators to an ocean of mud. Also at this year's festival were Motorhead, Slash, Rage Against the Machine, Megadeath and AC/DC amongst many others.

After Download Aerosmith played London's O2 Arena before they travelled to Greece, Romania, the Netherlands, and Belgium, where they played Graspop Metal Meeting. Graspop is the Belgian heavy metal festival held in Dessel each year since 1996. Despite the small size of the festival grounds (upholding a perimeter of only approximately 4 km) the festival draws a large number of international spectators well in excess of 100,000. Aerosmith again headlined, with Motorhead, Slayer, Stone Temple Pilots and Saxon all on the bill. They next performed in Spain, France, the Czech Republic and Italy at the Heineken Jammin' Festival. The event in Milan has attracted attendances of more than 100,000 over the course of the three-day event; at this year's event on July 3rd 2010, Aerosmith again headlined, with Thirty Seconds to Mars, Pearl Jam and Green Day. However Green Day's planned performance was cancelled due to heavy snow flooding the stage.

The tour so far had gone perfectly without incident or any kind of illness or malfunction. It was here however, when the tour reached North America, that trouble once more flared up with Aerosmith. This leg of the tour commenced in July with problems

124

starting in August when Steven Tyler accidentally hit Joe Perry in the head with his microphone stand at a show in Wantagh, New York. During the show in Toronto, Joe Perry bumped into Steven Tyler causing him to fall off the stage. Joe Perry suffered a minor head injury at the Wantagh show and Tyler had to be helped back up by fans and Joe Perry himself at the Toronto show; despite this both shows went on. Around the same time as these incidents, tension again rose between the pair when it was announced that Steven Tyler was to become a talent judge on *American Idol*. Joe Perry criticised Steven Tyler, claiming that he didn't consult the rest of the band about the decision and that he found out on the Internet, like the rest of the world. According to Joe Perry nobody else in the band knew anything about it. It was on August 18th that it was reported that Tyler officially signed on with the show. Tom Hamilton did an interview at the time and claimed that he believed Steven Tyler had the time and energy to continue fronting the band while also being a judge on *American Idol* simultaneously. The band still planned to record a new album and on November 5th, 2010, Brad Whitford said the recording sessions would probably move to Los Angeles, where *American Idol* is headquartered, and then another world tour would follow.

The tour concluded on September 16th 2010 and despite the minor onstage issues and the backstage fallouts the tour was another incredible success for Aerosmith. It again topped the worldwide tours, this time for 2010, and was reported to have grossed US $36.4 million with a total attendance well in excess of 478,192 fans.

The band continued with every intention of completing their new album despite the solo projects that were now in place. Steven Tyler had songs ready to go and so did Joe Perry. It was simply a matter of getting them all together and committed to recording. Again, although the band decided to release another album, while this was planned, a compilation was released, entitled *Tough Love: Best of the Ballads*. The album was announced on March 30th 2011, and was released on Geffen Records on May 10, 2011. The album, as the name suggests, is a compilation of ballads the band had written spanning their career, the listing as follows: 'Angel' written by Steven Tyler and Desmond Child, 'Amazing (orchestral edit)' written by Steven Tyler and Richie Supa, 'Love in an Elevator (single version)' written by Steven Tyler and Joe Perry, 'Cryin' written by Steven Tyler, Jo Perry, and Taylor Rhodes, 'What It Takes' written by Tyler, Joe Perry and Desmond Child, 'Rag Doll' written by Steven Tyler, Joe Perry, Jim Vallance and Holly Knight, 'Crazy' written by Steven Tyler, Joe Perry and Desmond, 'Deuces Are Wild' written by Steven Tyler and Jim Vallance, 'Livin' on the Edge' written by Steven Tyler, Joe Perry and Mark Hudson, 'Blind Man' written by Steven Tyler, Joe Perry and Taylor Rhodes, 'Janie's Got a Gun (single version)' written by Steven Tyler and Tom Hamilton and 'Dream On' written by Steven Tyler.

Many felt that the album was intentionally designed to coincide with Steven Tyler's newly appointed position on *American Idol* as a judge on the show. In fact, the album was released just weeks before the close of the season and looked like it was directly pitched at the *American Idol* audience. The album is more of a greatest hits package, paying homage to the incredible comeback the band made in the late 1980s and early 1990s when the power ballad catapulted them into the mainstream charts. Although the compilation has the word ballad in the title this is a little sketchy; tracks such as 'Love in an Elevator' and 'Rag Doll' are not in this genre. Despite this it again raised the notoriety of this incredible ever changing and forever volatile rock band.

Shortly after the release of *Tough Love* the band announced they would tour Latin America in the autumn of 2011 and shortly afterwards they stated finally that they would be soon returning to the studio to produce their new album. It would be scheduled to be released in 2012 and again produced by Jack Douglas.

The new tour was titled simply The Back on the Road Tour. It was scheduled to play for eighteen shows in Latin America and Japan in late 2011, from late October to early November. Again, they played in territories that they hadn't played before, this time in Ecuador and Paraguay. They also performed in Panama for the first time in their career. The Japanese section of the tour marked the band's first performances in Japan in seven years.

While Aerosmith adjusted the set list significantly from show to show, a typical set list would look like this: 'Draw the

Line', 'Same Old Song and Dance', 'Mama Kin', 'Janie's Got a Gun', 'Livin' on the Edge', Joey Kramer drum solo, 'Rag Doll', 'Amazing', 'What it Takes', 'Last Child', 'Stop Messin' Around' or 'Combination'. These performances of the songs 'Combination', 'Stop Messin' Around', and 'Red House' featured Joe Perry on lead vocals. A brief snippet of the unreleased song 'Meltdown' was played as an intro to 'Red House' at the first Tokyo show. Following on was 'I Don't Want to Miss a Thing', 'Cryin' and finally 'Sweet Emotion'. For the encore the band typically played 'Dream On' 'Love in an Elevator' and 'Walk This Way'; however there was no encore in Lima, with no official explanation. Aerosmith performed anywhere between 16 and 21 songs at each concert. Steven Tyler had also been performing the first part of 'Home Tonight' solo on the piano before performing 'Dream On'. At the shows in Bogotá, Fukuoka, and Osaka, part of 'You See Me Crying' was played as an intro, and at the show in Hiroshima and the second show in Tokyo, part of his solo single 'Love Lives' was performed as an intro. A portion of 'Come Together' was played before 'Walk This Way' at the Osaka show.

The tour started on October 22nd 2011 at Lima in Peru at The Stadium of the National University of San Marcos, which holds over 70,000 fans. It then moved on to Paraguay. This show in Asunción Paraguay was postponed a day after Steven Tyler sustained facial injuries; this was reported to be when he fell in his hotel room shower, which was explained as a bout of food poisoning that dehydrated him, causing him to faint. Concerts in Argentina, Brazil, Panama, Colombia, Ecuador and Mexico followed, where the band played three concerts: November 8th in Mexico City, 10th in Zapopan and on 12th at Monterrey. The Asian leg commenced on November 22nd at Kanazawa before shows in Hiroshima, Tokyo, Fukuoka, Osaka, Nagoya and finally Sapporo which concluded the tour on December 10th.

Moving into 2012, Aerosmith featured on an episode of *60 Minutes*. The show is basically an American news magazine and television programme broadcast on the CBS television network. It made its debut back in 1968. The special on Aerosmith featured interviews with the band members, who spoke very openly about each other, interspersed with footage from live shows throughout

127

2011. This naturally sent rumours again circulating regarding a rift between the band members; however, this was put to bed when Joe Perry surprised Steven Tyler by performing 'Happy Birthday' for him on *American Idol*, on March 22nd 2011. It was billed as an early birthday present for him.

Shortly afterwards, on March 26, Aerosmith announced a summer tour with Cheap Trick to be entitled the Global Warming Tour. On May 23, Aerosmith debuted their new single, 'Legendary Child', on the season finale of *American Idol*, and naturally this came with huge exposure for the band. Shortly after, they announced that their fifteenth studio album would be called *Music from Another Dimension!* and it would be released on November 6, 2012.

'Legendary Child' was selected as the lead single and released on May 24th 2012 just before the start of the planned tour. It wasn't a new song, as it had originally been written and recorded in 1991 during the initial sessions for the *Get a Grip* album, but was never officially released. On closer inspection fans had spotted that there a small part of it, in the form of an instrumental, played during the Pump Tour in 1990 as part of the 'Sweet Emotion' medley with the 'Peter Gunn Theme', so the song was clearly being played with as the band toured and continued to play live. As a result, the track was re-worked and now released as a lead single to the new album. In addition, the song also appeared in the film *G.I. Joe: Retaliation*. The movie had an initial planned release for the summer of 2012, but it was postponed and eventually released a year later on March 28th 2013. Shortly after Aerosmith debuted 'Legendary Child' on the final of *American Idol*, the song was made available for digital download and premiered on various radio stations.

With the single now out the new tour started on May 30th 2012; it would go right through until June 2014. The Global Warming Tour would include 82 scheduled concerts covering North America, Oceania, Asia, Latin America, and Europe.

The stage remained similar to that of past tours the band had embarked upon. The main stage itself had the classic Aerosmith logo painted on top and two small platforms off to each side. Kramer's drums were at the back, Hamilton and Whitford were on the left side, and Perry was on the right side. The back-up musicians were at the back-left of the stage behind a stack of amps. In the middle of the main stage was the catwalk, which ran through a full nine rows at each venue. At the end of the catwalk was a B-stage, which ran through the tenth row to the sixteenth row. Around the entire stage was a half-metre wide barricade that contained security and a few select fans. The show was the usual brilliant full dramatic spectacle. It typically started with a video playing on the main video screen that was reminiscent of the original opening from *The Outer Limits*. Near the end of the video, smoke would rise from the end of the B-stage and from the main stage. When the video finished, Kramer, Whitford and Hamilton would kick into the opening song, while Tyler and Perry would rise from a trapdoor at the end of the B-stage before the show went into full concert mode with Aerosmith playing like only they can: captivating, rocking and in full control over the presentation of their incredible back catalogue. There were several encores as the tour went on, and at a few venues a third encore was even played, either 'Mama Kin' or 'Chip Away the Stone'. When the encores wrapped up, a few cannons fired silver confetti into the audience. After the confetti storm, Tyler would introduce the back-up musicians (Taylor, Abair and Irwin) and the members of Aerosmith. Finally, he would hand the microphone to Perry, who would introduce Tyler. After the introductions, the band would walk out with 'Mannish Boy' by Muddy Waters playing over the speakers.

Before the actual tour commenced the band played a private event for Walmart shareholders on May 30th 2012. The first leg included 23 performances and lasted from late May through early August 2012. The second single from the new album was now released, 'Lover Alot', on August 22nd 2012. The song was premiered on radio stations throughout North America a week before being released as a single. The single 'What Could Have Been Love' was also released on August 22nd 2012. The power ballad also had a video that the band released later in October on Vevo.com. The song premiered live on November 8th 2012 at the Chesapeake Energy Arena in Oklahoma City, Oklahoma. Later still in November 2012 the song charted at number seven on the Japan Billboard Japan Hot 100 Chart alongside the actual release

129

of the album. The following year, on January 25th 2013, it was announced that the song would be coming to *Rock Band 3* as downloadable content along with five other Aerosmith songs as part of the 'Aerosmith's Greatest Dimension' pack. The pack was released on January 29th 2013.

Also in August 2012 Aerosmith released a video with bassist Tom Hamilton on their official YouTube channel, asking fans which artwork he should choose for their second single, 'What Could Have Been Love'. Both 'Lover Alot' and 'What Could Have Been Love' were released on radio simultaneously on August 22 and on the iTunes Store on August 28. Also on August 28, a revised track list consisting of 15 songs was released and on August 31st Joey Kramer premiered 'Street Jesus' on an Austin, Texas radio station, where it was largely well received by hardcore fans.

The set list for the first leg was different to the second leg of the tour. The first leg had the set list of: 'Draw the Line', which was switched to 'Toys in the Attic' on August 10th, 'Love in an Elevator', 'Oh Yeah', 'Lick and a Promise' played only on July 21st, 'Livin' on the Edge', 'Cryin'', 'Jaded' played on various occasions, 'S.O.S. (Too Bad)' replaced with 'Come Together' later on the tour, 'Last Child, Joey Kramer drum solo, 'Rag Doll' and sometimes 'Lord of the Thighs', 'Boogie Man'/ instrumental jam, 'Theme from Peter Gunn' played on some dates, 'Combination', 'What It Takes', replaced later with 'Stop Messin' Around', 'Rattlesnake Shake', 'No More No More' replaced later with 'Stop Messin' Around', 'Legendary Child', 'Rats in the Cellar'/'I Don't Want to Miss a Thing' or 'Falling in Love (Is Hard on the Knees)' were also played in this spot, 'Walking the Dog' /'Chip Away the Stone'/ 'Big Ten Inch Record' were also played here, Tom Hamilton bass solo, 'Uncle Salty' which was played only partially, 'Sweet Emotion', 'Mother Popcorn' which was played only on selected nights, 'Walk This Way', 'Dream On', 'Train Kept A-Rollin'' and 'Mama Kin' which again was played on selected dates.

Before the second leg started the band performed a brief set at the iHeartRadio Music Festival in mid-September. In addition to this they also began promotion of their new album, which was now imminent. They played various TV appearances with performances in New York City and did a special performance in front of their old Boston apartment.

The second leg also toured North America, starting in September and running through until December 13th in Nashville. This included a total of 14 performances through November and December 2012. This also coincided with the release of the new album, which was now scheduled for November 6th 2012.

North America 2 began in Las Vegas on September 22nd. The band then played New York at the Hurricane Sandy event, titled Hurricane Sandy: Coming Together. This was a one-hour TV special that was a commercial-free benefit concert. It was aired simulcast in the United States on November 2, 2012. The special raised money for the relief efforts for the aftermath of Hurricane Sandy, which had struck the US Northeast four days earlier. All proceeds from the concert went to the American Red Cross. In October 2012 *Rolling Stone* premiered the track 'LUV XXX'. They then premiered the entire album, track-by-track, leading up to the album's release. However, there was a major leak of the album on October 17th. *Rolling Stone* had uploaded all of the songs to their media player without placing any type of protection on them, which resulted in the entire fifteen songs on the regular edition of the album circulating around on the Internet.

Also in October, as part of Pepsi's NFL Anthems project, Aerosmith released a rewritten version of 'Legendary Child' which had the slightly changed title of 'Legendary Child - Patriots Anthem'. The lyrics had been reworked as a tribute to the New England Patriots. The song was made available for free download on the Pepsi Anthems website. Continuing on with the main tour the band played on November 5th in Boston before the long-awaited release of *Music From Another Dimension!*.

Music From Another Dimension! was unique for Aerosmith in the fact that the recording was split over many years and many sessions. The album was recorded from July 5th 2011 to March/April 2012 at various studios over various stages. The studios were Pandora's Box, The Boneyard, Poppy Studios, Swing House Studios, Mad Dog Studios, Spitfire Studio, Retro Activ Studios, Briar Patch Studios and Hensen Studios. The album's actual release was six years since Aerosmith last released original material. The two tracks 'Devil's Got a New Disguise' and 'Sedona Sunrise', were previously released as part of the band's compilation album *Devil's Got a New Disguise* back in October 2006. Also, it had been eight years since the band's last studio album, the mostly blues cover album *Honkin' on Bobo* which also included the lone original song 'The Grind', released in March 2004. It had been in fact a full eleven years since the band's last all-original studio album, which was *Just Push Play*, released back in March 2001.

The final track listing was 'LUV XXX' written by Steven Tyler and Joe Perry, 'Oh Yeah' written by Joe Perry, 'Beautiful' written by Steven Tyler, Marti Frederiksen, Brad Whitford, Joey Kramer and Tom Hamilton, 'Tell Me' written by Tom Hamilton, 'Out Go the Lights' written by Steven Tyler and Joe Perry, 'Legendary Child' written by Steven Tyler, Joe Perry and Jim Vallance, 'What Could Have Been Love' written by Steven Tyler, Marti Frederiksen and Russ Irwinr, 'Street Jesus' written by Steven Tyler, Brad Whitford and Joe Perry, 'Can't Stop Lovin' You' (featuring Carrie Underwood) written by Marti Frederiksen, Steven Tyler, Brad Whitford, Joey Kramer and Tom Hamilton, 'Lover Alot' written by Steven Tyler, Marti Frederiksen, Joe Perry, Tom Hamilton, Brad Whitford, Joey Kramer, Jesse Kramer and Marco Moir, 'We All Fall Down' written by Diane Warren, 'Freedom Fighter' written by Joe Perry, 'Closer' written by Steven Tyler, Marti Frederiksen and Joey Kramer, 'Something' written by Joe Perry and 'Another Last Goodbye' written by Steven Tyler, Desmond Child, and Joe Perry.

There were many reports about the album itself with speculation that the band had been working on it since 2006, but it remains unknown how much of the album was actually recorded over the period from 2006 through to the 2012 release date. They did also release a few trailers for the release of the album; the first was in August 2012 on YouTube, which included pro-shot live footage which was possibly from the upcoming bonus DVD for the album. It had interviews with the band, scenes of the band inside the studio, and snippets from the recent single 'Legendary Child'. The second followed in September, when they released a trailer for the album on Vimeo. The beginning of the video was made to look like a comic book with pictures of Aerosmith recording and discussing the album. The new song, 'LUV XXX' was playing in the background. The video then transferred into a room where the band and producer, Jack Douglas, were tossing around ideas. It then cut to several studio clips of the band rehearsing and recording the album with a commentary by Tom Hamilton. Around a week later a third trailer was released, again on Vimeo. The preview started off with Joe Perry and the producer, Jack Douglas, in the studio discussing a song from the upcoming album, then it cut to the same opening as in episode one. It then featured discussions about guitar riffs before a video of the band at Vindaloo Studios with a voice-over commentary by Joey Kramer; the commentary lasted for two more clips. The second to last clip was of the band discussing a few songs in an office with Jack Douglas; this also included Steven Tyler playing guitar.

The album was naturally long awaited and upon release it went straight in at number five on the Billboard 200. However, this was no longer the way to fully gauge success. In 2012 chart positions and numbers were largely irrelevant and continue to be so to this day. The chart system was broken into so many pieces the only way you could really gauge a band's popularity was on tour. It was here that there was literally no one to touch Aerosmith as they continued through North America.

The tour continued on November 8th in Oklahoma City and Wichita on November 11th at The Intrust Bank Arena. They next played Kansas, Austin, New York City at Madison Square Garden, Atlantic City, Columbus and then Canada with a concert in Toronto at The Air Canada Centre on November 27th. Moving into December they played Las Vegas, Los Angeles, New Orleans, Sunrise, Tampa and Nashville. The first two legs were held primarily in indoor arenas, with a couple of outdoor shows and a few festivals on the first leg, including three in eastern Canada and Milwaukee's Summerfest.

Before the third leg of the tour Aerosmith released 'Can't Stop Lovin' You', featuring Carrie Underwood, in January 2013. It was the fourth single from *Music from Another Dimension*. The track was released as a digital download single.

The third leg of the tour ran from late April to mid May 2013 and saw Aerosmith playing their first shows in Australia since 1990, as well as their first shows in New Zealand and the Philippines. This section started in Sydney on April 20th 2013, and the band then played New Zealand before returning to Australia with concerts in Brisbane and Melbourne.

Significantly, on April 17th 2013 it was announced that Steven Tyler and Joe Perry would be inducted into the Songwriters Hall of Fame at a ceremony to be held on June 13th.

Continuing the tour, they played through the Philippines, Indonesia and Singapore throughout May, concluding on May 25th 2013. Back in the US, on May 30th 2013, they again played another charity concert, this time at Boston Strong, which was a concert for victims of the Boston Marathon bombings which occurred on April 15th of this year. In July 2013, the band played at the Greenbrier Classic in West Virginia and at Foxwoods Resort Casino in Connecticut.

In July the band released the live concert DVD *Rock for the Rising Sun*, which documented the band's 2011 tour of Japan. The release was also screened in select theatres later in the year in October. As well as documenting the Japanese tour in 2011 it was also at the aftermath of the devastating earthquake and tsunami that struck the country earlier that year. The DVD includes documentary footage of the band as they travel the country and interact with fans. The Japanese version of the DVD featured four additional live tracks. *Rock for the Rising Sun* was a huge hit and debuted straight in at number one on Billboard's Top Music Videos Chart.

A month after the release of the DVD, now sitting at number one around the world, the band continued the successful connection with Japan, performing four concerts, at Chiba City, Nagoya and Osaka for two shows on August 14th and 16th.

Aerosmith's worldwide popularity and their incredible live shows continued in earnest. The next leg toured Latin America, starting in September 2013 at Venezuela before they rocked through Costa Rica, El Salvador, Guatemala, Uruguay, Argentina and Brazil, including headlining the Monsters of Rock Festival on October 20th 2013. They finally finished this leg with a concert in

Mexico at Mexico City at the Arena Ciudad de Mexico October 27th 2013.

Starting in May 2014 the tour reached Europe with a concert in Istanbul, Turkey. It then commenced through Bulgaria, Lithuania and Russia with two shows, Moscow on May 24th and Saint Petersburg on May 27th. Finland, Sweden, Norway, Denmark and Germany followed, with a concert at the O2 Arena in Berlin on June 9th 2014. They then played Poland before again playing the Download Festival in beautiful Leicestershire, England, on June 15th 2014. Aerosmith again headlined the festival, and alongside them this year were Linkin Park, Status Quo, The Offspring and Joe Bonamassa amongst many more.

They returned to Germany shortly after for a concert at Dortmund before they played in France at the Hellfest Festival. The festival's high attendance gives it the largest turnover of all French music festivals; in addition it is one of the biggest metal festivals in Europe and the first to ever exist in France itself. They next played a concert in Italy before concluding again in England at Clapham Common on June 28th 2014. The Festival, also known as Calling Festival, was a new version of Hard Rock Calling and wrapped up another incredible tour and a statement from a rock band that was simply unmatched in its continuity, ferocity and output around the world.

The stats yet again were incredible for the band; they again topped the list of successful tours for North America in 2012, with a reported total gross income of $31 million, and an estimated attendance of over 300,000 fans, over the 33 concerts. The Global Warming Tour in support of *Music from Another Dimension* had again covered the planet with sell-out shows in North America, South America, Asia, Oceania and Europe. The tour started on May 30th 2012 and went through until June 28th 2014 covering eight legs. It played a total of 82 concerts with 46 in North America, 5 in Oceania, 6 in Asia, 7 in South America and 15 in Europe. It solidified Aerosmith once again as one of the world's greatest, if not the greatest, touring rock bands.

Aerosmith continued touring, and moving further into 2014 announced that they would be again hitting the road in North America with Slash, along with Myles Kennedy and the

Conspirators. The tour would go through the summer. This would follow a 17-date European tour that Aerosmith performed from May 14 to July 2. The North American tour, known as the Let Rock Rule Tour, sent Aerosmith to 21 locations from July 10 to September 12 of this year. In October of 2014 Joe Perry released his autobiography entitled *Rocks: My Life in and Out of Aerosmith*. The book was co-written by David Ritz. He promoted the book with a book-signing tour that took him to 14 locations across the United States throughout October. Moving into 2015, Aerosmith premiered the film *Aerosmith Rocks Donington* in February. It appeared in 300 movie theatres across North America; the concert video is from the band's 2014 performance at Download Festival at Donington Park in Leicestershire, England. The video was released on DVD/Blu-ray later in the year, in September.

The band continued their individual solo projects, and in March 2015 Steven Tyler announced that he was working on his first solo country album. He signed a deal with Scott Borchetta's Dot Records, which is a division of the Big Machine Label Group. He released the lead single 'Love Is Your Name', and promoted the song on the *Bobby Bones Show*, iHeartMedia, *CBS This Morning, Entertainment Tonight* and also on the *American Idol* season 14 finale. Solo projects aside, Aerosmith didn't wait long to return to what they do best. On June 10th 2015 they embarked on the Blue Army Tour. The tour travelled through North America with many concerts played in smaller venues and in areas the band would not normally play in, areas where they had either never performed or had not performed in for many years. They also played a one-off show in Moscow on September 5. They also played many lesser known songs on the tour.

Once the tour was finished Steven Tyler completed work on his solo album, *We're All Somebody from Somewhere*. It was released on July 15, 2016. Prior to the album's release, a second single, 'Red, White & You', was released in January 2016, followed by the third single, which was the title track, in June 2016. The album was a success for Steven Tyler. It debuted at number one on the Top Country Albums chart and debuted at number 19 on the Billboard 200.

Also, in 2015 Steven Tyler launched Janie's Fund, obviously named after 'Janie's Got a Gun'. It provided protection and counselling for young female victims of abuse. He has gone on to help raise over $2.4 million for the organisation since then, including funds for Janie's House, which was established in 2017 in Atlanta. The house offers shelter for the victims of abuse or neglect, with space for 30 live-in clients and 24-hour medical facilities.

After the band members again worked on various side projects, they reconvened for a festival performance in San Diego on September 17 2016. They then embarked on another tour, this time focusing on Latin America. They called it the The Rock 'N' Roll Rumble Tour. The band performed at a mix of large outdoor festivals, stadiums, and arenas. The tour started in the US at the Kaaboo Festival, then moved on to Columbia, Chile, two dates in Argentina, and three concerts in Brazil, Peru and Mexico, ending the 10 dates on October 27th 2016.

Starting in April 2017 the band decided to tour again, with many speculating, including the band themselves, that it could be their last. The tour was to be called The Aero-Vederci Baby! Tour and it was planned to last for upwards of three years. The tour started with a free show in Phoenix, Arizona and took the band through Europe and South America. They performed in the country of Georgia for the first time in their career. The tour was planned to cover Europe, North America, Middle East and South America. It started on April 2, 2017 and ended officially on May 5, 2018. There were five legs scheduled with 25 shows: three in North America, sixteen in Europe, four in South America, and two in the Middle East. Four shows were cancelled along the way due to Steven Tyler having health problems. As before, along the tour the band also headlined many festivals; these included The March Madness Music Festival on April 2nd 2017, The Sweden Rock Festival on June 8th, The Download Festival on June 11th, Hellfest in France on June 17th, Firenze Rocks Festival in Italy on June 23rd, Rock Fest BCN on July 2nd in Barcelona and The New Orleans Jazz and Heritage Festival which took place on May 5th 2018. Shortly after the tour was scheduled to finish, the band announced that Aero-Vederci Baby! was not really a final tour and they will be touring again in 2019, to celebrate their 50th anniversary.

It is here on the 50th anniversary of this incredible band that we catch up with them within these pages, pages that highlight the incomparable achievements of one of the world's greatest and most influential rock bands. Aerosmith are pure rock and roll, the very essence of what it is all about. Their legacy is well documented and secure and their achievements will be forever admired. They continue to this day, rocking stadiums around the world and staying true to what they ultimately are: a truly incredible live rock and roll band.

Legacy and Achievements

The stats for Aerosmith are truly remarkable for a single rock band. They are the biggest selling American hard rock band of all time, having sold more than 150 million records worldwide. This includes over 70 million records in the United States alone. They have achieved 25 gold albums, 18 platinum albums, and 12 multi-platinum albums and hold the record for the most total certifications by an American band and for the most multi-platinum albums by an American band. They have released twenty-one Top 40 hits on the Billboard Hot 100 and have had nine number one Mainstream Rock hits. They have four Grammy Awards, six American Music Awards, and ten MTV Video Music Awards. They were inducted into the Rock and Roll Hall of Fame in 2001, and were included among both *Rolling Stone*'s and VH1's lists of the 100 Greatest Artists of All Time. And of course, both Steven Tyler and Joe Perry have both been inducted into the Songwriters' Hall of Fame. In 2019 the band will receive a star on the Hollywood Walk of Fame. According to SoundScan they have sold over 31,702,000 albums since 1991 when SoundScan started tracking actual sales figures, and this number is still rising.

Aerosmith's own influences in the early days were bands such as the Beatles, the Rolling Stones, the Yardbirds, Led Zeppelin, and the New York Dolls, particularly on the early circuits and clubs they were playing, building a following. They would of course go on to outgrow all other hard rock bands, and as a result they became hugely influential themselves. Van Halen for example started out by playing Aerosmith songs on the LA club circuit; but this was only the tip of the iceberg for the influence they would continue to have both live and on record. You don't have to look far to find Aerosmith's influence on future generations of hard rock and heavy metal bands. The list is huge but includes Mötley Crüe, Guns N' Roses, Skid Row, Extreme, Warrant, Inglorious, the Black Crowes, as well as Metallica, Metal Church, and Testament. Guns N' Roses in particular are a standout. Slash himself has often said that Aerosmith is his favourite band. Many bands cite Aerosmith as one of the main reasons they started a band and play rock and roll; and Steve Tyler as a rock and roll front man is considered one of the greatest of all time. The list continues of bands naming Aerosmith as their main influence: James Hetfield identifies Aerosmith as having been his main musical influence as a child, and has said they were the reason he wanted to play guitar, and even members of alternative rock bands such as Nirvana, Mother Love Bone/Pearl Jam, Stone Temple Pilots, Staind and Godsmack are self-professed early Aerosmith fans.

From a musical standpoint the brilliant interplay between Joe Perry and Brad Whitford has been greatly inspiring to many bands, especially Guns N' Roses. Joe Perry himself has received widespread recognition and praise as a lead guitarist, and has shared the stage many times with Jimmy Page and Jeff Beck, who Perry cites as a primary influence. Jimmy Page himself asked Steven Tyler and Joe Perry to induct Led Zeppelin into the Rock and Roll Hall of Fame. During the ceremony in 1995, Steven Tyler and Joe Perry delivered their speech, and they then joined the band onstage for a brief set. Joe Perry and Jimmy Page also were invited to play at Beck's and Metallica's induction in 2009. They performed a set comprising of the Yardbirds/Zeppelin/Aerosmith classic 'Train Kept A-Rollin'.

Their influence has not just stayed within the genre. Such is Aerosmith's popularity and musical standing they have crossed the divide into other areas, making them hugely influential in American and worldwide culture as a whole. They have collaborated with popular non-rock artists, such as Run-DMC, Eminem ('Sing for the Moment'), and Carrie Underwood, and performed with N Sync, Britney Spears, Mary J. Blige, and Nelly for the Super Bowl XXXV halftime show. Country artists Garth Brooks and Mark Chesnutt both scored hit singles with covers of

140

Aerosmith songs; Brooks in 1995 with 'The Fever', a reworking of Aerosmith's 1993 song, and Chesnutt in 1999 with a cover of Aerosmith's 1998 song 'I Don't Want to Miss a Thing'. The barriers that were once there within hard rock bands were shattered with Aerosmith with the release of 'Walk This Way' with Run-DMC. They crossed the line and opened up rock music to a new generation that gained access to them and their incredible back catalogue.

They are a band that truly epitomises everything that is rock and roll. They were not alone in the early excesses that they famously pursued. Others such as Led Zeppelin, the Stones and countless others were allegedly involved in this scene with the now infamous recording sessions for 1976's *Rocks* and 1977's *Draw the Line* especially noted for their substance indulgence, including heroin. They had limited resources, but they were without doubt the most potent, rebellious and turbulent rock 'n' roll band in that era. In the mid to late 1970s, the band enjoyed tremendous popularity in the United States and in Japan, though they failed to make a big impression in Britain. Still, they were among the most popular hard rock acts in America in the late 1970s, along with Heart, Kiss, Ted Nugent, ZZ Top, and Boston. Their massive popularity fell back briefly during the departures of both Joe Perry and Brad Whitford, but their return to success after they had cleaned up was under the circumstances beyond remarkable. Their return has been often described as 'the single most successful comeback in the history of heavy metal', if not all of popular music.

Aerosmith's tours are also an achievement behind comparison. And the shows they performed were gruelling. They gave electrifying performances night after night, and they did it the hard way by building themselves up from the small clubs in their local area to fully sold out world tours and festival headliners. The tours they performed in the 1970s and the 1987–1995 era numbered in the triple digits in numbers of dates, headlining or co-headlining festivals along the way, such as the Texxas Jam in 1978 and 1987, the Monsters of Rock festival at Castle Donington, England in 1990 and 1994, and Woodstock '94. The band became infamous for their touring and remain one of the greatest and most captivating live bands on the planet. In addition they received numerous awards for pioneering expansive, conceptual music videos, such as those for 'Janie's Got a Gun' (directed by future *Fight Club* director David Fincher), 'Livin' on the Edge', 'Cryin'', 'Amazing', 'Crazy', 'Falling in Love (Is Hard on the Knees)', and 'Pink'. Aerosmith shattered musical barriers in all aspects; nothing was out of bounds for them and they embraced everything that came their way. They were one of the bands to take this crossover even further and pioneered rock music in gaming, capturing even more fans along the way, introducing themselves in new and ingenious ways. They appeared in the *Grand Theft Auto* series, with some games entirely dedicated to the band, like *Quest for Fame* and *Revolution X*. Aerosmith was the first band to have its own *Guitar Hero* title, *Guitar Hero: Aerosmith*, which is considered to be the best-selling band-centric video game across both the *Guitar Hero* and *Rock Band* platforms. Many ageing rock stars and rock and roll bands fall out of favour very easily with the younger generation, the next generation. It's very easy to look at the stars of the 1970s, 80s and 90s now and see why the younger generation would not be interested. They look the same, wear the same clothes and essentially play the same songs. Aerosmith shattered all this; it was and is always cool to like Aerosmith. They moved with the times, crossed barriers and constantly reinvented themselves. They produced new music consistently and kept adding to the list of live staples to perform when they embarked on record breaking world tours. They never once became uncool or out of touch with either their existing core fan base or the new generations that saw or heard them for the first time.

Remaining at the top of the music world when starting in the early 1970s is an incredible achievement on its own. Add in unlimited access to anything a young band wanted, drugs, alcohol, women and a life touring clubs and bars, then this achievement is even more remarkable. In fact, it's remarkable that the band are even alive, let alone still performing at the highest level in 2019. The level of change that has come around in music from the 1970s would have been inconceivable to bands at that time. The way we consume music now has changed rapidly and it changed constantly along the way. Bands that were not up for the change quickly fell out of favour and many got left behind. Aerosmith started in the clubs, built a following as a brilliant live band but essentially ripped themselves apart. Their comeback embraced culture and from that point whenever culture changed Aerosmith were there; they never really suffered, they rolled with it, embraced it and stayed completely culturally relevant. And this is the main difference: where other bands had their four or five years at the top and then dropped back, Aerosmith kept going. They kept adapting and kept changing, but in a way that stayed true to what they ultimately are.

This is why the Bad Boys from Boston are without doubt one of the greatest rock and roll bands in the history of rock music.

19: Discography

There is a huge discography attributed to Aerosmith: below is a brief synopsis of their listing...

Aerosmith:
Steven Tyler – lead vocals, harmonica, percussion, piano, keyboards (1970–present)
Tom Hamilton – bass (1970–present)
Joey Kramer – drums, percussion (1970–present)
Joe Perry – lead and rhythm guitar, backing vocals (1970–1979, 1984–present)
Brad Whitford – rhythm and lead guitar (1971–1981, 1984–present)
Former members
Ray Tabano – rhythm and lead guitar (1970–1971)
Jimmy Crespo – lead and rhythm guitar, backing vocals (1979–1984)
Rick Dufay – rhythm and lead guitar (1981–1984)

Studio Albums:
Aerosmith (1973) Released: January 5, 1973 Label: Columbia
Get Your Wings (1974) Released: March 15, 1974 Label: Columbia
Toys in the Attic (1975) Released: April 8, 1975 Label: Columbia
Rocks (1976) Released: May 14, 1976 Label: Columbia
Draw the Line (1977) Released: December 9, 1977 Label: Columbia
Night in the Ruts (1979) Released: November 16, 1979 Label: Columbia
Rock in a Hard Place (1982) Released: August 27, 1982 Label: Columbia
Done with Mirrors (1985) Released: November 4, 1985 Label: Geffen

Permanent Vacation (1987) Released: August 25, 1987 Label: Geffen

Pump (1989) Released: September 12, 1989 Label: Geffen

Get a Grip (1993) Released: April 20, 1993 Label: Geffen

Nine Lives (1997) Released: March 18, 1997 Label: Columbia

Just Push Play (2001) Released: March 6, 2001 Label: Columbia

Honkin' on Bobo (2004) Released: March 30, 2004 Label: Columbia

Music from Another Dimension! (2012) Released: November 6, 2012 Label: Columbia

Live Albums:

Live! Bootleg Released: October 27, 1978 Label: Columbia

Classics Live! Released: April 7, 1986 Label: Columbia

Classics Live! II Released: June 1, 1987 Label: Columbia

A Little South of Sanity Released: October 20, 1998 Label: Geffen

Rockin' the Joint Released: October 25, 2005 Label: Columbia

Aerosmith Rocks Donington 2014 Released: September 4, 2015 Label: Universal Music Group

Compilation Albums:

Greatest Hits Released: November 11, 1980 Label: Columbia

Gems Released: November 15, 1988 Label: Columbia

Pandora's Box Released: November 19, 1991 Label: Columbia

Pandora's Toys Released: June 8, 1994 Label: Columbia

Big Ones Released: November 1, 1994 Label: Geffen

Box of Fire Released: November 22, 1994 Label: Columbia

Classic Aerosmith: The Universal Masters Collection Released: November 2, 2000 Label: Geffen

Young Lust: The Aerosmith Anthology   Released:
November 20, 2001 Label: Geffen

O, Yeah! Ultimate Aerosmith Hits Released: July 2, 2002
Label: Columbia/Geffen

Devil's Got a New Disguise: The Very Best of Aerosmith
Released: October 17, 2006 Label: Columbia

20th Century Masters: The Millennium Collection – The
Best of Aerosmith Released: November 6, 2007 Label: Geffen

Tough Love: Best of the Ballads Released: May 10, 2011
Label: Geffen

The Essential Aerosmith Released: September 13, 2011
Label: Columbia

Tours:
1970–1972: Club Days
1973: Aerosmith Tour
1974: Get Your Wings Tour
1975: Toys in the Attic Tour
1976–1977: Rocks Tour
1977–1978: Aerosmith Express Tour (supporting *Draw the
Line* album)
1978: Live! Bootleg Tour
1979–1980: Night in the Ruts Tour
1982–1983: Rock in a Hard Place Tour
1984: Back in the Saddle Tour
1985–1986: Done With Mirrors Tour
1987–1988: Permanent Vacation Tour
1989–1990: Pump Tour
1993–1994: Get a Grip Tour
1997–1999: Nine Lives Tour
1999–2000: Roar of the Dragon Tour
2001–2002: Just Push Play Tour
2002: Girls of Summer Tour
2003: Rocksimus Maximus Tour
2004: Honkin' on Bobo Tour
2005–2006: Rockin' the Joint Tour
2006: Route of All Evil Tour
2007: World Tour 2007

2009: Guitar Hero: Aerosmith Tour
2010: Cocked, Locked, Ready to Rock Tour
2011: Back on the Road Tour
2012–2014: Global Warming Tour
2014: Let Rock Rule Tour
2015: Blue Army Tour
2016: Rock 'N' Roll Rumble Tour
2017–2018: Aero-Vederci Baby! Tour
2019: Aerosmith: Deuces are Wild

Extended Plays:
Vacation Club (1988)
Made in America (1997)

Films:
Aerosmith:
1978 Sgt. Pepper's Lonely Hearts Club Band - Future Villain Band
1988 The Decline of Western Civilization Part II: The Metal Years - Themselves
1990 Saturday Night Live: Musical guests; 'Wayne's World' sketch - Themselves
1991 The Simpsons: Flaming Moe's episode - Themselves (voices)
1993 Wayne's World 2 - Themselves
1993 Saturday Night Live: Musical guests; Bad Dancer sketch - Themselves
1997 Saturday Night Live: Musical guests; Mary Katherine Gallagher sketch - Themselves
2001 Saturday Night Live: Musical guests - Themselves
2005 Be Cool - Themselves
Steven Tyler Specifically:
1978 Sgt. Pepper's Lonely Hearts Club Band - Member of the Future Villain Band
1988 The Decline of Western Civilization Part II: The Metal Years - Himself
1990 Saturday Night Live: Musical guest; Wayne's World sketch - Himself

1991 The Simpsons: Flaming Moe's episode - Himself (voice)

1993 Wayne's World 2 - Himself

1993 Saturday Night Live: Musical guest; Bad Dancer sketch - Himself

1997 Saturday Night Live: Musical guest; Mary Katherine Gallagher sketch - Himself

1999 Clubland - David Foster

2001 Saturday Night Live: Musical guest - Himself

2002 Lizzie McGuire - Father Christmas/Himself

2004 The Polar Express - Elf Lieutenant / Elf Singer

2004 Goodnight Joseph Parker - Sammy

2005 Be Cool - Himself

2003–2006 Two and a Half Men - Himself; two episodes

2009 Chris Botti In Boston - Himself

2010 The Wonder Pets: Adventures in Wonderland - the Mad Hatter

2011 American Idol - Himself (judge)

2013 Ke$ha: My Crazy Beautiful Life - Himself; Episode: A Warrior in The Making

2013 Epic - Nim Galuu (voice)

2013 Miss Universe 2013 - Himself

2013 Top Gear - Himself

2014 Hell's Kitchen - Himself; Episode: 11 Chefs Compete, Part 2

2015 Nashville - Himself

Soundtracks:

'Come Together' - Sgt. Pepper's Lonely Hearts Club Band soundtrack (1978)

'Rocking Pneumonia and The Boogie Woogie Flu' - Less Than Zero soundtrack (1987)

'Love Me Two Times' - Air America soundtrack (1990)

'Dream On' - Last Action Hero soundtrack (1993)

'Deuces Are Wild' - The Beavis and Butt-Head Experience (1993)

'Dude (Looks Like a Lady) (live)' and Shut Up and Dance (live)' - Wayne's World 2 soundtrack (1993)

'I Don't Want to Miss a Thing', 'What Kind of Love Are You On', 'Sweet Emotion', and 'Come Together' - Armageddon soundtrack (1998)

'Angel's Eye' - Charlie's Angels soundtrack (2000)

'Theme from Spider-Man' - Spider-Man soundtrack (2002)

'Lizard Love' - Rugrats Go Wild soundtrack (2003)

'Sweet Emotion' - Starsky & Hutch soundtrack (2004)

'Walk This Way' - Sex and the City: The Movie soundtrack (2008)

Video Games:
1994 Revolution X
1995 Quest for Fame
2008 Guitar Hero: Aerosmith

About the Author

Growing up through the 1980s James was surrounded by the Pop hits of the day and soon became fascinated with the Pop stars and Musicians that played through the TV and Radio. Here he started searching for something more satisfying and moved through to soul music, jazz, and rhythm and blues. It was Funk however that really got James's attention and from here he never looked back. James Brown, Sly and the Family Stone, Parliament and Prince all captured this perfectly. James loved the way that these groups and individuals brought together a strong melody, chord progressions, rhythmic groove of a bass line and drums. All these factors were then for the first time brought to the foreground. Funk was found and once discovered, James was hooked. James started writing extensively on Prince through various platforms and it wasn't long before he had amassed a significant stockpile of material worthy of a Biography. Over the years James has collected an enviable catalogue of Prince Vinyl Records, CDs, Tapes, Cassette, DVDs and Memorabilia. The Biography was finally completed in 2018, and has been nominated for the 2019 Association for Recorded Sound Collections Awards for Excellence in Historical Recorded Sound Research. James is delighted to have joined New Haven Publishing and has added to his music icon series, aptly titled The Life The Genius The Legend, with Lenny Kravitz (releases April 29 2019) and Madonna (releases August 30th 2019)

CPSIA information can be obtained
at www.ICGtesting.com
Printed in the USA
LVHW080106171219
640694LV00007B/317/P

9 781912 587278